821.17
z-biL

CHAUCER'S
LEGEND OF GOOD WOMEN

THE CHARACTER AND RELATIONS
OF THE MANUSCRIPTS

THE PROLOGUES

SOME DOUBTFUL READINGS

AMS PRESS
NEW YORK

CHAUCER'S LEGEND OF GOOD WOMEN

THE CHARACTER AND RELATIONS
OF THE MANUSCRIPTS

THE PROLOGUES

SOME DOUBTFUL READINGS

BY

J. B. BILDERBECK, M.A. (Cantab)

PRINCIPAL AND PROFESSOR OF ENGLISH,
THE PRESIDENCY COLLEGE,
MADRAS, S. INDIA

For wel I wot that folk han here be-forn
Of makynge ropyn and lad a-wey the corn,
I come aftyr glenynge here and ther
And am ful glad if I may fynde an er (L.G.W.)

LONDON:
HAZELL, WATSON & VINEY, Ld.
52, LONG ACRE, W.C.
1902

Library of Congress Cataloging in Publication Data

Bilderbeck, James Bourdillon.
 Chaucer's Legend of good women.

  1. Chaucer, Geoffrey, d. 1400. Legend of good women.
PR1882.B5 1972   821'.1   78-39441
ISBN 0-404-00859-3

Reprinted from the edition of 1902, London
First AMS edition published in 1972
Manufactured in the United States of America

AMS PRESS INC.
NEW YORK, N. Y. 10003

SYNOPSIS OF THE DISSERTATION

Part I. The Character and the Relations of the MSS. of the "Legend of Good Women"

PAGES

Sect. i. Collation of four Manuscripts—G.F. R A. 1–33
        (*a*) Unique readings examined of G. . . . 4–13, 26–29
                                    F. . . 13–22, 26–29
                                    R. ⎫
                                    A. ⎭ . . . 23–29
        (*b*) Examination of readings
             in which MSS. pair   G.F.—R.A. . . 29, 30
                                         G.R.—F.A. ⎫
                                         G.A.—F.R. ⎭ . . 30–32
        (*c*) Summary of the results of the Collation . . 32, 33
Sect. ii. Evidence of the revision of the Legends stated
            and discussed 34–42
       No evidence of revision of Legends of
            Philomene, Phyllis, Hypermnestra . . . 42–44
Sect. iii. (*a*) Description of the various authorities
           for the text of the L.G.W. . . G. 45–7   F.B.T. 48–54
                                   A. 54–58   R. 58–60
                                   α. 60–62   γ. 62–65
                                   β. 65–67   P. 67–68
                                 Rl. 68–69 Ff. 69, 70
                                 Th. 70, 71
        (*b*) Unsatisfactory character of the MSS. . . . 71–74
        (*c*) Order of the Legends 74
        (*d*) Summary of the results obtained—A
            critical text 74–76

Part II. The Prologues to the "Legend of Good Women"

Sect. i. Which of the Prologues is the earlier? 77–83
Sect. ii. The circumstances out of which the L.G.W.
        arose 83–91
Sect. iii. The plan of the Poem 91–93
Sect. iv. Dates of composition of the Prologues and
        the Legends . . . . . , 93–109

Appendix. Some doubtful readings 110–114

Texts of the "Legend of Good Women" consulted or examined.

Manuscripts. Gg. 4. 27 } Cambridge University Library.
Ff. 1. 6

R. 3. 19 Trinity College Library, Cambridge.

Pepy's, 2006, Magdalen College Library, Cambridge.

Fairfax, 16
Tanner, 346
Bodley, 638 } Bodleian Library, Oxford.
Arch. Selden, B. 24
Rawlinson, C. 86

Additional MS., 9832,
Additional MS., 12,524, } British Museum.
Additional MS., 28,617,

Printed Texts. The Chaucer Society printed copies of the above MSS. in—

A Parallel-Text Edition of Chaucer's Minor Poems,

Supplementary Parallel-Texts of Chaucer's Minor Poems,

A One-Text print of Chaucer's Minor Poems,

Odd Texts of Chaucer's Minor Poems.

Thynne's Edition of 1532, as reprinted by the Chaucer Society in *A Parallel-Text Edition of Chaucer's Minor Poems.*

The Complete Works of Geoffrey Chaucer, Vol. III., by W. W. Skeat. Oxford, 1894.

The Complete Works of Geoffrey Chaucer, Vol. I., by T. R. Lounsbury. New York, 1900.

Authors or Works quoted or referred to in the dissertation.

Bech, M.   *Anglia*, Vol. V., 365-380.
Brink, B. ten.   *Chaucers Sprache und Verskunst.* Leipzig, 1899.
    Chaucer. Studien zur Geschichte seiner Entwicklung und zur Chronologie seiner Schriften. Munster, Leipzig, 1870.
    Englische Studien, xvii., 13 ff. Leipzig, 1892.
    History of English Literature, 1883-1893. Bohn's Standard Library.
Court of Love.   In Vol. VII. of *The Complete Works of Geoffrey Chaucer*, by W. W. Skeat.
Dictionary of National Biography.   Articles on Anne, John of Gaunt, Edmund de Langley, Michael de la Pole, Richard II., Robert de Vere, Thomas of Woodstock.
Furnivall, F. J.   *A Temporary Preface to the Six-Text Edition of Chaucer's Canterbury Tales;* Part I. Chaucer Society, 1868.
    Trial Forewords to my " Parallel-Text Edition of Chaucer's Minor Poems." Chaucer Society, 1871.
Gower, John.   *Confessio Amantis*, edited by R. Pauli. London, 1857.
    The Complete Works of John Gower, edited by G. C. Macaulay. Oxford, 1899, *etc.*
Hollis, Thomas and George.   *The Monumental Effigies of Great Britain.* London, 1840.
Kaluza, Max.   *Englische Studien*, xxii., p. 281.
Koch, John (of Berlin).   *The Chronology of Chaucer's Writings*, 1890. Chaucer Society, Second Series, 27.
Köppel, Emil.   *Englische Studien*, xvii., pp. 195-9.
Kunz, Siegfried.   *Das Verhältnis der Handschriften von Chaucers " Legend of Good Women "*—Inaugural Dissertation. Berlin, 1889.
Legouis, Émile.   *Quel fut le premier composé par Chaucer des deux Prologues de la Légende des Femmes exemplaires?* Le Havre, 1900.

Authors or Works quoted or referred to

Lounsbury, T. R. *Studies in Chaucer, his life and writings.* 3 Vols. London; New York, 1892.

Macaulay, G. C. *The Complete Works of John Gower.* 3 Vols. 1899, *etc.*

Manly, J. M. *Observations on the Language of Chaucer's "Legend of Good Women."* Cambridge, Mass.—Harvard University Modern Language Departments, Studies and Notes, *etc.*

Nicolas, Sir Harris. *Proceedings and Ordinances of the Privy Council of England,* Vol. I., 1834.

Rymer's *Fœdera,* Vol. VII. London, 1709.

Sandford, Francis. *A Genealogical History of the Kings and Queens of England.* London, 1707.

Shaw, Henry. *Dresses and Decorations of the Middle Ages, from the 7th to the 17th Centuries.* 2 Vols. London, 1843.

Skeat, W. W. *The Complete Works of Geoffrey Chaucer.* 7 Vols. Oxford, 1894, *etc.*

Stanley, A. P. *Historical Memorials of Westminster Abbey.* London, 1882.

Stow, John. *Annales, or Generall Chronicle of England.* London, 1615.

Stubbs, W. *The Constitutional History of England.* Library Edition. Oxford, 1880.

Walsingham, T. *Historia Anglicana,* edited by H. T. Riley. 2 Vols. London, 1863.

Wright, T. *Political Poems and Songs relating to English History.* 1859.

CHAUCER'S 'LEGEND OF GOOD WOMEN.

Part I.—The Character and Relations of the Manuscripts.

The first part of this dissertation will be devoted to an examination of the character and relationships of the extant MSS. of the *Legend of Good Women* and of Thynne's printed edition (1532) of the poem, copies of all of which have been printed by the Chaucer Society under the editorship of Dr. F. J. Furnivall. This subject has already been investigated by Siegfried Kunz in his inaugural dissertation entitled, *Das Verhältnis der Handschriften von Chaucers "Legend of Good Women,"* and to a partial extent by Prof. W. W. Skeat, who gives his deductions on pp. xlvii.-li. of his introduction to the poem in Vol. III. of the *Works of Geoffrey Chaucer*. As a result of my own investigation, I find I am not in a position to accept all the conclusions of these writers.

I append a list of the texts examined, which, for the sake of brevity and convenience, will be referred to in this dissertation by the letters placed against them:—

Cambridge University MS. Gg. 4. 27.	G.
Fairfax MS. 16, Bodleian Library	F.
Tanner MS. 346, Bodleian Library	T.
Trinity College, Cambridge, R3. 19.	R.
MS. Arch. Seld. B.24, Bodleian Library	A.
Thynne's Edition, 1532.	Th.
Bodley MS. 638, Bodleian Library	B.
Pepys' MS. 2,006, Magdalen Coll., Cambridge	P.
Additional MS. 9,832, British Museum.	α
Additional MS. 12,524, British Museum	β
Additional MS. 28,617, British Museum	γ
MS. Ff. 1. 6. Cambridge Univ. Library	Ff.
Rawlinson MS. C.86, Bodleian Library	Rl.

Section i.—Collation of G.F.R.A.

As a preliminary step to the investigation of the nature and relations of the extant MSS. copies of the *Legend of Good Women*,

a collation of G.F.R.A. was undertaken, and a detailed analysis *
of the agreements and variations in reading among them was prepared for every line of the legends. These four MSS. were selected, because they all present a nearly complete copy of the legends, and seemed to be—what as a matter of fact they are—fairly representative of the different classes of texts, in manuscript or in print, that have been published by the Chaucer Society under the editorship of Dr. Furnivall.

I may mention *in limine* that, in determining agreements for the purposes of this analysis, I decided to neglect all such variations as were due to the existence of obvious *minor* errors of scribes (chiefly mis-spellings), to the insertion of an unnecessary *e* final, to the insertion or omission of *n* final as part of the verbal inflexion *en*, and to the omission in the spelling of a word of a sonant *e* whether as an inflexion or an integral part of a word in Chaucer's system of pronunciation. When such errors affect the metre of a line, the MS. exhibiting an error is marked as defective, but the errors are not regarded as invalidating the agreement between this defective reading and a sound one in another MS. Without doubt, such small variations are important in helping us to estimate the qualifications of a scribe, the relative age and value of MSS. transcriptions, or even their relations to one another; but, as one of the main objects of this inquiry was to arrive at a knowledge of Chaucer's actual language from a comparison of MSS., some of which are of late date, it was important to observe the extent to which they confirmed one another, and consequently to make such allowances as might be made without running the risk of misinterpreting readings. That such a course of inquiry was possible, is proved by the existence of this dissertation; that it was useful, must be demonstrated by the results obtained.

It should be here stated that in this discussion, for the sake of brevity and convenience, agreements between MSS. will be represented by placing the letters indicating the MSS. side by side. Further, when a MS. shows a line in some way defective, the letter indicating the MS. will generally be printed in italic, and when such an italic letter is found associated with another letter in roman, it implies that the MSS. indicated by these letters

* Not printed.

are in harmony in respect to the particular matter under consideration. To illustrate these statements: F.R.A. indicates that the three MSS. agree in a certain reading; G.R. *ornementis* implies that G. and R. both agree in the reading indicated, but that R. is defective. Moreover, when two or more MSS. are shown as being in agreement, the reading, if given, is generally quoted from the MS. first indicated.

The collation above referred to demonstrates :—

(1) that in a large majority of lines all *four* or *three* of the MSS. collated are in substantial agreement;

(2) that in lines in which a particular reading is supported by only two MSS., agreements between G. and F. are far the most common ;

(3) that F.R.A. each present numerous unique readings, and that, though in most cases these unique readings are obviously corrupt, or on examination are found to be unsound, they in some cases appear to be satisfactory in sense, grammar, and metre ;

(4) that G. also is frequently unique in its readings, and that, though some of these unique readings are corrupt, there are many others which appear to be thoroughly sound ;

(5) that, among the four MSS., G., as the least corrupted, is decidedly the best authority for the text, and that F. ranks next.

As an investigation of the unique readings of the MSS. seemed likely to yield most useful results in determining the values and the relations of the MSS., I compared these unique readings in each MS. with the corresponding readings in the others—

(*a*) in cases in which one MS. presented one reading (not obviously unsound) and *three* others agreed in another reading ;

(*b*) in cases in which one MS. presented a unique reading (not obviously unsound) against a different reading presented by *two* other MS. ;

(*c*) in cases in which all the MSS. differed from one another (obviously unsound readings being excluded).

I now reproduce, in full, lists showing the variations referred to in (*a*) and (*b*), so far as G. and F. are concerned. In respect to R. and A, only partial lists will be presented. Lists showing the variations referred to in (*c*) will also be given, very slight variations in reading being omitted.

G.—F.R.A.

The following list exhibits the unique readings of G. against the readings of F.R.A.:—

603	G. nas to hym no thyng	F.R.A. was nothing to him
636	G. peynede	F.R.A. peynen
671	G. wolde	F.R.A. wol
694	G. ben wel sene	F.R.A. wel be sene
725	G. and Tysbe heit (highte) te (the) maide Naso seyth thus	F.R.A. all om. *and*
738	G. cop	F.R.A. top (*N.B.* T.=G.)
773	G. on a day that	F.R.A. on a day whan
780	G. And to begile here wardeynys echon	F.R.A. And to begile hire wardeyns everychone
784	G. wolde	F.R.A. sholde
794	G. And so gret haste Piramus to se (P.Ff. = G.)	F.R.A. And (F. Had) so grete lykynge Piramus to see (*N.B.* T. And)
798	G. and	F.R.A. for
845	G. that	F.R.A. the
856	G. Be comyn hider and may me not I-fynde	F.R.A. Be comen hider and may me nat fynde
874	G. medeled	F.R.A. medeleth (A. mellith)
882	G. he	F.R.A. she
883	G. is	F.R.A. was
890	G. myn	F.R.A. thy
895	G. felawe and cause of	F.R.A. felawe and cause eke of
920	G. for	F.R.A. to
932	G. Feynynge the hors I-offerede to Mynerue	F.R.A Feynyng the hors offred unto Mynerve (R. ffeyned)
960, 961	*in G. only*	
1003	G. schule, the longe while	F.R.A. wolde (wold); F.A. to longe (A. long) while; R. to long awhile
1006	G. than is the	F.R.A. om. *is* to the violation of the metre
1025	G. the wal	F.R.A. a walle
1074	G. he semed	F.R.A. him semed
1082	G. and	F.R.A. she (R.A. sayd)
1094	G. Sche manye a beste to the shippis sente	F.R.A. Ful many a beste (R. best) she to the (R.A. hys) shippes sente
1102	G. of	F.R.A. and
1112	G. ffor his ese and for to take his reste	F.R.A. To take his ease and for to haue his reste (rest)
1119	G. shynede	F.R.A. shyneth; F.R. defective in metre; A. ins. *the* before *mycht* (*N.B.* T. shyned*e*)
1129	G. hadde sent	F.R.A. hath sent (F.R. *to* for *into*)
1135	G. presentis	F.R.A. presentynge
1149	G. thankyth; with good entente	F.R.A. thanked; in good intente (F. om. *ful*)

1170	G. leue	F.R.A. dere
1171	G. slep	F.R.A. dreme
1173	G. Me thynkith that he is so wel I-wrought	F.R.A. For that (R. om.) me thinketh (A. think) he is so wel y-wrought
1178	G. if that ye rede it me	F.R.A. yif that (R. om.) ye rede me
1187	G. for no thing	F.R.A. for no wyght
1193	G. his	F.R.A. hire
1235	G. chaunge hire for	F.R.A. chaunge for
1247	G. as his wyf	F.R.A. to hys wyfe
1283	G. of othere landys than of Cartage quien	F.R.A. of other lande than of Cartage a (A. the) queene
1313	G. His thral his seruant in the leste gre	F.R.A. Hys thral hys seruant in the lest (A. leste) degree
1314	G. to-fore	F.R.A. to foot
1389	G. ffor euere as tendere a capoun et the fox	F.R.A. For ever as tender a capon eteth the fox
1391	G. As shal the goode man that therefore hath payed	F.R.A. As shal the good man that ther-for payed
1405	G. of fredom and of strenthe and lustynes	F.R.A. of fredome of strength and of lustynesse
1427	G. men may se	F.R.A. men myght see (F. *ther* for *therin*)
1462	G. seylith	F.R.A. sayled (*salt* for *salte*)
1482	G. to refrosche and for to	F.R.A. to refresshen and to (R. refresshe)
1514	G. And Ercules that hadde tho gret los	F.R.A. And Ercules that hadde (R.A. had) the grete los
1541	G. whiche a lusty lyf	F.R.A. suche a lusty lyfe
1626	G. I am	F.R.A. am I
1639	G. lef or loth	F.R.A. lef ne loth (F. leeve, R. lese)
1640	G. shulde neuere hire	F.R.A. shulde hir neuer (R. om. *ne*)
1660	G. weddyth	F.R.A. wedded
1677	G. fful meche ontrouthe hadde deyed with the	F.R.A. Ful mykel untrouthe had ther dyed with the
1684	G. ne telle I nat	F.R.A. om. *ne*
1688	G. for	F.R.A. that
1701	G. no more	F.R.A. om. *no*
1702	G. and that	F.R.A. om. *and*
1717	G. Nor at the yote porter nas there non	F.R.A. Nor at the gate porter was ther noon
1718	G. And at the chambre dore they gan abyde	F.R.A. And at the chambre dore they abyde
1725	G. seyth men	F.R.A. sayne men (*N.B.* T.=G.)
1727	G. so longe	F.R.A. to longe
1734	G. And mekely hyre eyen let she falle	F.R.A. But mekely (F. mekly) she let hir eyen falle
1749	G. nas	F.R.A. was
1752	G. is	F.R.A. was
1753	G. ffor he woste wel she wolde not ben getyn	F.R.A. For wel thoghte he she shulde (R.A. wold) nat begeten
1754	G. And ay the more that he was in dispayr	F.R.A. And ay (R. euer) the more he was in dispaire
1756	G. This	F.R.A. Hys
1762	G. thus	F.R.A. this (thys)

1786	G. the	F.R.A. this
1788	G. What beste quod she is that weyeth thus	F.R.A. What best ys that quod (R. quoth) she that weyeth thus
1812	G. Romeyn wyuys	F.R.A. Romaynes wyfes
1813	G. here shame	F.R.A. the shame
1815	G. loste at onys bothe	F.R.A. loste both atones (R.A. lost)
1821	G. worthi knyght	F.R.A. werray knyght
1826	G. Whan this was gon and this myschaunce befalle	F.R.A. Whan he was (A. is) goon, al (R.A. and) this myschaunce ys (R. was) falle (R.A. fall)
1830	G. wemen usyn tho	F.R.A. wymmen used tho
1836–1907 *wanting in G.*		
1911	G. caughte hyre herte	F.R.A. caste hir hert (R.A. cast)
1919	G. in sorwe and in distresse	F.R.A. in sorowe and distresse (*N.B.* T.=G.)
1922, 1923 *wanting in G.*		*found in* F.R.A.
1933	G. as it fil aboute	F.R.A. as it cam (com) aboute (R. *castyd* for *casten*)
1948	G. and forth is gon	F.R.A. and forth is lad (R.A. yong)
1978	G. leue systyr Phedra dere	F.R.A. Phedra leve suster dere
1984	G. how so euere we do	F.R.A. how so that we do
1996	G. the	F.R.A. this
2009	G. and slen hym as	F.R.A. to sleen (sle) hym or
2027	G. And whan	F.R.A. Whan (*N.B.* This gives a monos. first measure)
2056	G. so wolde god	F.R.A. as wolde god (R. god wold)
2064	G. than mote falle	F.R.A. ther moten falle (F.R. mot, F. *dede* for *dethe*)
2134	G. oughte her-of us	F.R.A. oughte us here-of
2142	G. the	F.R.A. this
2188	G. I am betrayed and al hire her to-rent	F.R.A. I am betrayed (A. betraised) and hir heer to-rent
2248	G. that cuntre	F.R.A. hir contree
2293	G. how so euere he do	F.R.A. how so that (R. om.) hyt goo
2294	G. And with hise wilis he so fayre hire preyede	F.R.A. And with his wiles kneled and so preyde
2324	G. By force hat he this traytour don that dede	F.R.A. By force hath (R. had) this traytour done a dede
2345	G. And swor (hir) that he say his sistyr ded	F.R.A. And swore hir (R. om.) that he fonde his suster dede
2365	G. systeris loue	F.R.A. suster love
2367	G. with	F.R.A. by
2396	G. wete if that like yow	F.R.A. fynde yf that hyt liketh (R. lyke) yow
2408	G. fful of his folk	F.R.A. Ful of folk (A. folkis)
2419	G. as ony torche it brende	F.R.A. as ony torche brende (R. brend)
2449	G. owene faderys	F.R.A. olde fadres
2480	G. Wel and homly and let his shippis dighte	F.R.A. Wel and homely and hys shippis dygh*te*
2500	G. that ye seyde	F.R.A. as ye seyde (A. *nyll* for *ne*)
2501	G. that	F.R.A. which
2505, 2506 *omitted in G.*		
2521	G. to fre	F.R.A. so fre

Chaucer's Legend of Good Women 7

2539	G. men (caught from 2537?)	F.R.A. folk
2546	G. with swich an art and with swich subtilete	F.R.*A*. With suche an arte and suche (A. suich) soteltee
2620	G. til an ende	F.*R*.A. to an ende
2676	G. a bedde	F.*R*.*A*. to bedde
2712	*G*. a ful gret pas	*F*.R.*A*. a ful good pas (A. space)

It is obvious that G. presents a large number of unique readings against F.R.A. The variations will be thus classified:—

1. *Substitutions* in—
    (*a*) articles and pronouns: 845, 882, 890, 1025, 1082* (and, she), 1193, 1541, 1756, 1762 (thus, this), 1786, 1813, 1996, 2142, 2248, 2500 (that, as), 2501;
    (*b*) prepositions: 920, 1102 (of, and), 1149, 1247 (as, to), 2367, 2620, 2676;
    (*c*) conjunctions: 773 (that, whan), 798, 1082* (and, she), 1102 (of, and), 1639, 1688, 2056, 2500 (that, as);
    (*d*) adverbs: 1727, 1762 (thus, this), 2064, 2521;
    (*e*) tenses and moods: 636 (G. corrupt?), 671, 784, 874, 883, 1003, 1129, 1149, 1427, 1462, 1660, 1752, 1830.

2. *Transposition of words*: 603, 694, 1626, 1640, 1815, 1978, 2134.

3. *Miscellaneous*—
    (*a*) Lines in which G. preserves an apparently sound reading, while F.R.A. are corrupt: 725 (spelling careless in G.), 890, 1006, 1074, 1119, 1313, 1391 (G., however, has *goode* for *good*), 1405, 1701, 2324 (G. *that* for *a*), 2480 (*homly* for *humbly*?).
    (*b*) Lines in which G. presents what seems to be a sounder reading than F.R.A.: 1389, 1514, 1677 (*ontrouthe* is accented on the second syllable), 1725, 1826 2027, 2408, 2449.
    (*c*) Lines in which there is little to choose between the readings indicated: 738, 794, 895, 1178, 1187, 1235, 1314, 1482, 1684, 1717, 1749, 1754, 1812, 1821, 1911 (G. in error?), 1919, 2293, 2345 (*fonde* for *say*), 2365, 2396 (*wete* for *fynde*), 2419, 2546, 2712.
    N.B. In lines 2345, 2396, G. is defective, and corruption may be suspected in 1178, 1235, 1911, 2539.

---

* Here G. *and* may be a copyist's slip, as *seyde* has no grammatical subject.

(*d*) Lines in which there is a substantial difference between G. and F.R.A., the readings of the latter showing what may be regarded as improvements: 780, 784, 798, 856, 932, 960, 961, 1094, 1112, 1135, 1170, 1171, 1173, 1283, 1702, 1734, 1753, 1788, 1922, 1923, 1933, 1948, 1984, 2009, 2188.

4. *Readings all doubtful* : 2294.*

An inspection of these lists shows that, in a large number of instances, the variations are, comparatively speaking, of an unimportant character. In some cases, without doubt it would be possible, in others it is impossible, to decide between the rival claims of these various readings whose existence, speaking generally, is undoubtedly owing to accident, negligence, or even the idiosyncrasies of scribes. Similar variations in which the differences are slight will be observed when the unique readings of F., R., and A., respectively, are treated. For the present purpose, such small variations will be set aside.

As regards Group 2—*Transposition of words*—in every instance, except 1815, the G. readings are inferior as to rhythm to the readings of the three other MSS., and are probably corruptions. A similar phenomenon reveals itself after examination of the unique readings of F., R., and A., and these facts appear to justify the adoption of this canon of criticism: that if one MS. presents an order of words which is different from the order found in two or more MSS. which are not closely related to one another, the unique reading is probably a corrupt reading.

If we next turn to the "*Miscellaneous*" group of various readings, two extremely interesting and important facts stand out very clearly. They are—

(1) that G. presents the only sound, or the most acceptable, reading in a large number of lines: see (*a*) and (*b*);

(2) that in many lines—see (*d*)—F.R.A. present readings which exhibit a marked improvement on the corresponding readings in G., though the latter in themselves appear to be sound enough, and would, in the absence of other authority, be accepted by scholars as Chaucer's own work.

In respect to the first of these facts, it has to be observed that

* See p. 43.

Chaucer's Legend of Good Women

similar phenomena reveal themselves in the analysis of the unique readings of F., R., and A., but that the examples offered by G. are far more numerous than those presented by the other MSS. This feature is an illustration of the superiority of the text in G., as being an older and a less corrupted copy of the poem.

As regards the second fact, I submit that, if G. presents an older and less corrupted text, and if, in the examples indicated above in *Miscellaneous* (*d*), the readings of F.R.A. are in various ways superior to the readings of G., while the latter appear to be sound enough in themselves, we are justified in accepting the conclusion that the changes must have been made by the author himself, or, in other words, that G. represents an earlier draft of the legends, while F.R.A represent a revised draft. This subject will presently receive fuller treatment.

G.—F.R.—F.A.—R.A.

The following list presents the unique readings of G. against the readings of the other MSS. when two of them are in agreement:—

587	G. To han the world unto	F.A. To haue the world at	R. To haue the world under	
623	G. . . . I wele lete slippe	F.R. . . . I wol let yt slyppe	A.	
716	G. . . . lond on of the lustyeste	F.A. . . . londe oon the lustieste	R. (*N.B.* T.=G.)	
718	G. That tho was in that lond estward dwellynge	F.R. That esteward in the worlde was tho dwellynge	A.	
730	G. . . . myghte nat assente	F.A. nold (A. wold*e*) yt not assente	R. wold nat assent	
750	G. that; that	F. the; the	R.A. that; the (*N.B.* T.=R.A.)	
831	G. herte (for *heer*?)	F.A. heer (hair)	R.	
870	G. tho	F.R. now	A.	
887	G. Tysbe ryst vp withoutyn ony bost	F.A. Tesbe rist vppe withouten (A. without) noyse or booste	R. Thys Tysbe ryseth without noyse or bost	
928	G. In Naso and Eneydos	F.R. In thyne Eneyde and Naso	A.	
938	G. lowe brought	F.A. lowe y-broghte	R. low brought	
944	G His owene fadyr I-clepid Anchises	F.R. His olde (old) fader cleped Anchises	A.	
963	G hadde take	F.A. had y-take	R. had take	
966	G. the cuntre for tespie	F.R. the contree for to spye	A. the contree to aspye (*N.B.* T.B.=G.)	

1009	G. That sche was holdyn alle queenys flour	F.R. That she was holde of alle (F. al) quenes floure	A.
1099	G. He neuere at ese was betyr in al hese lyve	F.A. He neuer better at ease was his lyve	R. He neuer better at ease was in his lyue
1107	G. of ornementis	F.A. of pavements	R. other ornamentes
1109	G. whan he hadde sete	F.A. whan that he hadde (A. had) seete.	R.
1115	G. to iuste	F.R. the iustyng	A. corrupt; supports F.R.
1160	G. now comyth	F.A. now to	R.
1175	G. And ek thereto so mech(e) good he can	F. And withal soo mykel good he kan	R.A. And therewithal so (A. as) moche good he can
1191	G. wolde	F.R. wol	A.
1203	G. That helith syke men of nyghtis sorwe	F.A. That heelith seke folkes (A. folk) of nyghtes sorwe	R. That heleth folkes of hyr nyghtys sorow
1212	G. The hirde of hertis is I-founde a-non	F.A. The heerde of hertes founden ys anoon	R.
1217	G. These bestys wylde	F. The wilde hertes	R.A. These wyld (wilde) bestys
1248	G. Swich sorwe as he makede	F.A. Swiche sorowe as he hath maked (A. maid)	R.
1259	G. Se ye nat alle how that ye (for *they*?) ben forsworn	F.R. Se ye nat alle (F. al) how they byn forsworn	A. See ye nat all how that thei be for-suorn
1267	G. trewe	F.R. privy	A. besy
1275	G. Synde hire letteres tokenys brochis ryngis	F.R. Send hir letres tokens broches and rynges	A.
1324	G. Mercy lord hauyth pete	F.R. Mercy lorde haue pitee	A. Now merci lord haue pitee
1330	G. Thus he hath left Dido in wo and peyne (for *pyne*)	F. And thus hath he lefte Dido in woo and pyne	R.A. And thus he left Dido in wo and pyne
1352	G. But yit as myn autour right thus sche seyde	F.R. But as myn auctour seythe yit thus she seyde	A. But as myn auctour seith ryght thus sche seid
1370	G. tendere; gentil	F. gentil; gentil	R.A. gentyl; tendre
1382	G. sekte	F. sleighte	R.A. set, sett
1423	G. Tho	F.A. So	R. Now
1438	G. Oetes	F.A. Otes	R. Otys
1449	G. Schis (Ches) what folk that thow wit (wilt) with the take	F.R. And chese what folk thou wilte wyth the take	A. And chese quhat folk that thow wilt with the take
1475	G. were thidyr blowe	F.A. thider were y-blow	R. thedyr were blow
1525	G. he hath hym vp areysid	F. he hath hyt vp reysed	R.A. he hath hym vpraysyd (A. vp raisit)

Chaucer's Legend of Good Women

1568	G. hire	F.R. his	A. *omits*
1570	G. coude	F.R. couthe	A. *omits*
1593	G. Oetes	F.A. Otes	R.
1597	G. doth; was	F. doth; is	R.A. dyd; was
1657	G. lefte hire	F. lefte	R.A. laft (left) hys
1659	G. as euere in loue a thef and traytour he was	F.A. And ever in love a cheve (A. cheif) traytour he was	R. And euyr in loue a thyef traytour he was
1779	G. hire lyght	F.R. hys lyght	A. hir sight
1813	G. ilke; here shame	F.A. thilke; the shame	R. that; the shame
1836–1907	*wanting in G.*		
1942	G. the	F.A. this (F. ys; A. was)	R.
1973	G. Hem leste nat to gone to bedde sone	F.R. Hem lest(e) nat to (F. om) go to bed so sone	A.
1977	G. This	F.A. Than	R.
1993	G. herte rote	F. hert rote	R.A. hertis rote
1999	G. and hath bothe room and space	F.R. and hath roome and eke space	A. and hath roum eke and space
2084	G. But synde yow grace of slyghte and hert also	F. And sende yow grace and sleyght of hert also	R.A. But send yow grace of hert and sleyght also
2184	G. hath now pete	F.	R.A. hath gret pitee
2208	G. rysith and kyssith	F.A. ryste and kyssed	R. rose and kyssyd
2266	G. but; must; with	F.R. but; moste (most); to	A. that; most; unto
2267	G. preyeth hym ho wolde	F.A. preyde hym that he wolde	R. prayed hym he wold
2350	G. lernede hadde	F. y-lerned had	R.A. lernyd hath
2358	G. coude	F.R. can	A. gan
2370	G. wolde	F.A. scholde (A. ins. *that*)	R. wold
2378	G. here alone	F.R. hir self allone	A.
2395	G. o wekid tre	F.R. of a wikked tree	A. of euill tree
2405	G. comyth	F.A. come	R.
2430	G. That to the deth he almost was I-drevyn	F.A. And to the dethe he was almoste y-dreven (A. dryuen)	R.
2445	G. of; the	F. in; hys	R.A. in; that
2469	G. don	F.A. doth	R.
2476	G. and hath hire sworn	F.R. and to hir swore	A. and hath to hire suorn
2509	G. comyth it noght	F. come hit noght	R.A. cometh nought
2534	G. That it mot be	F. That hyt be now	R.A. That it may be
2563	G. clepid	F.R. called	⎫
2579	G. shal	F.R. shulde	⎬ 2551–2616 *wanting in A.*
2598	G. That made hire for to turne (for *dye*) in prisoun	F.R. That made hir to dye in prison	⎭
2601	G. al thow	F.R. and thogh	
2632	G. myn ypermystre doughter	F.	R.A. Ipermystra my doughter

2639	G. ful	F.A. ryght	R.
2656	G. to bedde go	F.R. to bed goo	A. to bed y-go
			(*N.B.* T.=A.)
2687	G. She rist yit vp	F.A. She ryst hir vp	R. She ryseth vp
2706	G. wepe (for *wep*)	F.A. wepte (wept)	R.
2717	G. Why ne haddist thow	F.A. Why ne hast thow	R. Why haddest thow

The above variations may be thus classified:—

1. *Substitutions* in—
    (*a*) pronouns and articles: 750 (R.A.), 1568 (F.R.), 1779, 1813, 1942, 1977 (this, than), 2445; (*b*) prepositions: 2445; (*c*) conjunctions: 2601; (*d*) adverbs: 870, 1423; (*e*) tenses and moods of verbs: 963, 1191, 1570, 2208, 2267, 2350 (G.—R.A.), 2358, 2370, 2405 (?).

2. *Tranpositions of words*: 1475, 2084, 2430, 2632.

3. *Miscellaneous*:
    (*a*) Lines in which G. presents the only sound or what is probably the correct reading: 587, 716, 966, 1009 (*queenys* is gen. plur.), 1107, 1109, 1217, 1275, 1324, 1382, 1438, 1525, 1593, 1973, 1993, 2350, 2378, 2469, 2476, 2706 (*wepe* in error), 2717.
    (*b*) Lines in which there is little to choose between the readings: 623 (G.—F.R.), 730* (G.—F.), 938 (G.—F.A.), 963 (G.—F.A.), 1248 (G.—F.A.), 1330, 1370 (G.—R.A.), 1449 (G.—A.), 1597 (G.—F.—R.A.), 1657 (G.—F.), 2184 (G.—R.A.), 2395 (G.—F.R.), 2509, 2534 (G.—F.), 2563, 2639, 2656 (G.—A.), 2687 (G.—F.A.).
    (*c*) Lines in which there is a substantial difference between the readings of G. and the other MSS., the latter showing superior readings: *718, 887, 928, 944, 1099, 1115, 1160, 1175, 1191, 1212,* 1259, 1267, 2579.

4. *Readings all doubtful*: 1203, 1352, 1659, 1999, 2598.

Here, as in the previous analysis, there are numerous lines in which the variations in readings are small. In some cases it is possible to decide between them; in others it would be idle to attempt this.

* Possibly the right reading is *nolde nat assente*, and the alteration from *might* to *nolde* is the author's.

Chaucer's Legend of Good Women

As regards the variations indicated in Group 2, the readings of G. in 1475 and 2430 seem to violate the rhythm, and should be rejected. G. may or may not present the correct reading in 2084, 2632; but I prefer the G. reading in the former line.

Turning to the entries under the head of *Miscellaneous*, we observe a repetition of the phenomena already noticed in the previous analysis. Section (*a*) offers a list of lines in which G. preserves the only sound or what is probably the correct reading. Section (*c*) presents a supplementary list of lines in which the G. readings appear to have undergone revision: see the lines the number of which is printed in italic figures. *N.B.* In lines 1259, 1267, 2579 we may suspect corruption in G.

F.—G.R.A.

The following list exhibits the unique readings of F. as against the corresponding readings shown in common by G.R.A.:—

704	G.R.A. wele, wyll, wole (A. *thus* for *so*)	F. wolde (*N.B.* T.B.=G.R.A.)
724	*G.R.A.* called (R.A. yong)	*F.* cleped (yong)
892	G.R.A. shal geve me	F. shall me yive (*N.B.* T.B.=G.R.A.)
973	*G*.R.A. cutted (G. cutte)	*F.* knytte (so B.) (*N.B.* T. kutted)
997	G.R.A. were	F. nere
1024	G.R.A. this	F. the (*N.B.* T.B.=G.R.A.)
1145	G.R.A. take	F. make
1151	*G.R.A.* these (R.A. new)	F. this (*N.B.* B. the)
1172	*G.R.A.* newe (R.A. new)	F. ilke
1179	G.*R.A.* wolde	F. wil
1194	G.R.A. In to	F. Vn-to
1202	*G.R.A.* as (G. *bright* for *faire*)	F. is
1256	G.*R*.A. maketh (A. in; G.R. to)	F. maked
1258	G.*R*.A. olde ensaumples (R. om. *han*)	F. ensamples olde (*N.B.* T. om. *olde*)
1268	G.R.A. obeysauncis	F. obeysaunce
1284	G.R.A. wele, wyll, wole	F. wolde
1327	G.R.A. on to	F. vpon
1347	G.R.A. thyng	F. thinges
1357	G.R A. make I	F. I make
1362	G.R.A. lese on yow a word	F. lese a word on yow
1386	G.R.A. wel betere loue and chere	F. wel better and gretter chere
1396	G.R.A. as Guido	F. and Ouyde
1397	G.*R.A.* kyng (R. hight*e*)	F. knyght
1406	G.R.A. fadiris	F. fader
1443	G.*R.A.* swiche a (A. befallen)	F. suche (*N.B.* T.B. such)
1448	G.*R*.A. cost (A. *wolde* for *wil*)	F. costes

1472	G.R.A. Where that the ship of Iason gan a-ryue	F. Where lay the shippe that Iason gan arryve
1519	G.R.A. most she spak	F. she spake moste (*N.B.* T.B.=G.R.A.)
1548	G.R.A. And Iason	F. Thise Iason (*N.B.* T.=G.R.A.; B. *as* for *and*, *any* for *ys a*)
1575	G.*R.A.* sufferede	*F.* suffreth (*al* for *alle*)
1578	G.*R.A.* ne	*F.* and (*N.B.* T.B.=G.R.A.)
1582	G.R.*A.* matier (mater)	*F.* nature (*N.B.* T.B. *matire*; F.T.B. *appeteth* for *appetiteth*)
1634	G.R.A. to the poynt ryght	F. ryght to the poynt
1642	G.R.A. here	F. there (so B.) (*N.B.* T.=G.R.A.)
1652	G.R.A. tresor	F. tresoures
1653	G.R.A. is she gon	F. she is goone
1668	G.*R.A.* ther (R. was, founde)	F. neuer
1706	G.*R.A.* sir (A. ins. *rycht*)	F. for (so B.) (*N.B.* T.=G.R.A.)
1747	G.R.A. shap	*F.* bounte
1773	G.R.A. alday (R. quoth)	F. alwey
1784	G.R.A. were it	F. whether
1785	*G.R.*A. come, came, com (G. swerd drawe, R. swerde draw, A. suerd ydrawin)	F. cometh
1791	G.R.A. there	F. thou
1795	G.R.A. poynt (A. unto)	F. swerde
1804	G.R.A. seyth	F. seyde

(*N.B. Lines* 1836–1907 *are wanting in* G.)

1928	G.R.A. hadde (had)	F. hath
1954	G.R.A. were depe (G. thus, R. thys, A. this)	F. depe were (*N.B.* T. om. *were*)
1962	G.R.A. in; to	F. to; of (*N.B.* T. to; to)
1969	G.R.*A.* Adryane that	F. that Adriane
1971	G.R.A. compleynynge (R. *a* for *the*)	F. compleynt
1991	G.R.A. this	F. the (*N.B.* T.=G.R.A.)
1997	G.R.A. ther	F. ther as
2008	*G.*R.A. achoked (G. *as* for *at?*)	F. asleked
2020	G.RA. drede (R. hys)	F. stede
2026	G.R.A. this	F. the
2030	G.R.A. sorweful man dampnede	F. sorwful man y-dampned
2032	G.R.A. wil (A. wole I)	F. wolde
2039	G.*R.A.* han (R.A. haue) so gret a grace	F. have suche a grace
2070	G.R.A. I euere	F. ever y (*N.B.* T. om. *I.*)
2073	G.R.A. nat ellis (A. *preye* for *seye*)	F. no more (*N.B.* T. *nat* for *no more*)
2079	G.R.A. answerde hym	F. om. *him*
2092	*G.*R.A. Than that I sufferede giltles yow sterve (R. gyltles yow to sterue, A. yow giltles to sterue)	F. Than that I suffred your gentilesse to sterue
2094	G.R.*A.* no profre (A. *to* for *unto*, G. nys, R.A. ys)	F. not profet (*N.B.* T.B. no profit)

2107	G.R.A. wil (var. sp.)	F. wolde
2111	G.R.A. for tacheue my batayle	F. for to taken by batayle
		(*N.B.* T. *tayle* for *batayle*)
2120	G.R.A. this	F. these (*N.B.* T.=G.R.A.)
2126	*G.R.A.* al (G. om. *now*)	F. and
2149	G.R.A. Whan he this (A. the) beste hath	F. Whan he hath thys beste (*N.B.* T.B.=G.R.A.)
2160	G.*R.A.* newe (R.A. new)	F. noble
2218	G.R.*A*. more telle (A. ins. *of*)	F. telle more
2221	G.R.*A*. ende I telle shal	F. ende tel I shalle
2229	G.R.*A*. this (A. fair)	F. the
2233	G.R.A. fyn	F. fende (so T.B.)
2285	G.R.*A*. of (A. *corrupt*)	F. for
2346	G.R.*A*. this (A. om. *sely*)	F. the (*N.B.* T.=G.R.A.)
2354	G.R.A. sothly; hadde (had)	F. shortly; hath
		(*N.B.* T. *sothely* as in G.R.A.)
2355	G.R.A. and	F. of
2435	G.R.A. to kepen	F. and kepen
2440	G.R.A. court	*F.* contree
2442	G.R.A. of Athenys	F. at Athenes
2444	G.R.A. of gret renoun	F. grete of renoun
2453	G.*R.*A. hir likith (R. *corrupt*)	F. and lyketh (*N.B.* T. her lyked)
2488	G.*R.A.* hire delyuere (R.A. ins. *that*)	F. delyuer hir
2495	G.R.A. two	F. tweyne
2525	*G.R*.A. pleyne	F. seyne
2530	G R.A. wil (var. sp.)	F. wolde

(*N.B. Lines* 2551–2616 *are missing in A.*)

2620	G.R.A. the (R. was dryuyn)	F. that
2626	G.R.A. lokyth (A. *blith* for *glad*)	F. loked (*N.B.* T.B.=G.R.A.)
2652	G.R.A. so it to me be	F. so hit be to me
2661	G.R.A. haue	F. make (*N.B.* T=G.R.A.)
2665	G.R.A. grauntyth (G. is, R. was, A. nys)	F. graunted
2709	G.R.A. a (R. lepeth, A. lepte)	F. the

Here are many slight variations, such as the substitution for one another of pronouns, articles, prepositions, and conjunctions, and also interchanges between the present tense and preterite of verbs. See 704, *1024*, 1151, 1179, 1194, *1256*, 1284, 1327, *1575*, 1785, *1804*, 1928, 1962, 1991, 2026, *2032*, 2107, *2120*, 2229, *2285*, *2346*, 2354, 2355, *2442*, 2530, 2620, 2626, 2665, 2709.

Besides these there are small variations in 724, 997, 1172, 1202, 1406, 1443, 1548, *1578*, 1652, *1706*, 1773, 1784, 1791, *2126*, *2160*, 2354, *2435*, *2453*, 2495, 2525, *2661*.

Now, in the case of all the MSS. under consideration, we find that the readings of one frequently differ from the readings presented in common by the three others, and it is easy to understand this, for the variations are found in points in which corruption is extremely likely to occur as the result of accident, negligence, or the idiosyncrasies of a scribe. In many of the examples* adduced, it would be easy to identify an instance of editing or a corruption in F. by a collation of its readings with the readings of B. and T., with which it is closely associated. In some of the examples,* there can be little doubt that, in view of the requirements of grammar, idiom or sense, the G.R.A. reading is sound, and the F. reading is unsound. In 1179 and 1406 there is something to be said in favour of the F. readings, but in the remaining instances (except where a comparison with B.T. may help us) it would be unwise to express a preference, for it would be difficult to support an opinion by adequate reasons. The fact that such MSS. as G.R.A. agree in a reading would certainly lead us to suspect the soundness of a different reading in F., and, as we have some confidence in rejecting the F. readings in *nineteen* of the examples above given, we, perhaps, should not be far wrong if we were to reject most of the others. At all events, there is no evidence in these doubtful cases that there was anything of the nature of emendation or revision in the direction of G.R.A. to F., or *vice versa*.

As regards the examples in which the variations involve a transposition in the order of words, there can be little doubt that Chaucer cannot be held guilty of such violations of rhythm as we find in the F. readings in 892, 1258, 1519, 1653, 1954 (*depe* is dissyllabic), 1969 (*Adriane* is accented always on the first and third syllables: see 1977, 2078, 2146, 2158, 2171, 2175, 2181), 2070 (*euer* is generally monosyllabic before vowels), 2149, 2221, 2444, 2488, 2652. Only in lines 1357, 1362, 1634, 2218 is there room for doubt, but even in these instances the transposition might have been due to a scribe, and offers no ground in support of the hypothesis that there may have been emendation one way or the other.

In respect to the remaining variations, F. must be held to be unsound in its readings in 973, 1268, 1347 (hypermetrical), 1396, 1582, 1642 (*there* does not rime with *y-fere*), 1747 (*bounte* does not suit the context, and makes the line hypermetrical), 2008,

---

* See the lines whose number is indicated by figures in italic.

2111, 2233 (misapprehension of sense), 2440 (*countree* must be a slip for *court*, to which it is that Theseus directs his way).

There remain a few cases for more detailed examination :—

1145   G.R.A. Be as be may, I *take* of it no cure.
        F. Be as be may, I *make* of yt no cure.

Here F.T.B.Th. stand by themselves; P.Rl.*a*. confirm G.R.A. The F. reading is alliterative, and may embody an emendation.

1386   G.R.A. ffor they schal haue wel betere loue and chere.
        F. For they shal haue wel better and gretter chere.

Th. = G.R.A. ; T.B. = F. ; and *a*. reads—

   ffor they shall haue bettyr loue and chere.

The reading of F.T.B. may have been edited to get rid of the repetition of *love* (see 1385, 1387); it is poor in rhythm.

1397   G.*R.A*. Ther was a *kyng*.   F. Ther was a *knyght*.

Th.*a*.γ. = G.R.A. ; T.B. = F.   As "Pelleus" had not been made king, the reading of F. is an improvement, but, as the weight of evidence is against this reading, it must be accepted with caution.

1448   G.*R*.A. And al the cost I wele myn seluyn make (R. myself, A. wold*e*).
        F. And al the costes I wole my selfe make.

T.B. *my self* for *myselfe* ; hence it is not improbable that, *self* being taken as a monosyllable, *cost* was altered into *costes* by some editor in order to secure the right number of syllables.

1472   G.R.A. Where that the ship of Iason gan a-ryue.
        F. Where lay the shippe that Iason gan arryve.

a. = G.R.A. ; γ.B.T.Th. = F.   The F. reading is open to suspicion, as it involves a use of *that* which it would be difficult to justify.

1668   G.R.A. That in hise dayis nas (R. was) ther non I-founde.
        F. That in hys dayes nas neuer noon y-founde.

Here F. shows an additional syllable ending in a consonant before the cesural pause. The reading is confirmed only by B.T.Th.

1795   G.R.A. And sette the poynt al sharp vp-on (A. vnto) hire herte.
        F. And sitte the swerde al sharpe vnto hir herte.

a.β.γ. *poynt*, but differ in the preposition ; T.Th. *swerd, on*; B. *swerde, vn-to*. There is little to choose between the readings.

1971   G.R.A. His compleynynge as they stodyn (A. stood) on the (R. a) wal.
       F. Hys compleynt as they stode on the walle.

T.B.Th.γ. *compleynt*; α.β. *complaynynge*. There is not much to choose between these readings if *stode* in F. be read as *stoden*.

1997   G.R.A. ffor in the prysoun ther he shal descende.
       F. For in the prison ther as he shal descende.

This and 1668 are the only instances in this list of an extra syllable other than *e* final occurring before the pause, in which it cannot be said decisively that F. is corrupt. On the other hand, several examples may be quoted from F. of readings in which a redundant syllable occurring in G. has been removed.

2020   G.R.A. . . . out of this (R. hys) *drede*. F. . . . out of this *stede*.

β.γ. = G.R.A.; T.B.Th. = F. *Drede* perhaps affords a better rime with *lede* (A.S. *lēdan*). The first *e* in *drede* (A.S. *drēdan*) was probably an open, and the first *e* in *stede* (A.S. *steda*) a close sound, but these two words rime together in *House of Fame*, 829, 30.

2039   G.R.A. Ye graunte me to han so gret a grace.
       F. Ye graunte me to haue suche a grace.

β.γ. *so gret a grace*; T.B.Th. = F. The F. reading seems inferior.

2073   G.R.A. And mercy lady I can nat ellis seye (A. preye).
       F. And mercy lady I kan no more saye.

β.γ.Th. confirm G.R.A.; B. = F. T. reads *I kan nat sey*, and this seems to give the key to the reading of F.B. On the hypothesis that the common ancestor of F.T.B. was defective in the same way as T., it is possible that some scribe inserted *more* and changed *nat* to *no* to amend the line.

2079   G.R.A. Answerde hym to his profre and to his chere.
       F. Answered to hys profre and to hys chere.

F. may be correct, but β.γ. = G.R.A.

2092   G. Than that I sufferede gilt(e)les yow sterve.
       F. Than that I suffred your gentilesse to sterue.

β. supports G., and R.A.γ. read *gyltles*, but seem corrupt; T.B.Th. = F. Here the F. reading may have been edited. Adriane's pity for Theseus is aroused in view not only of his rank, but of the fact that he is guiltless (see 1979-1982). The correct reading is, without doubt., that of G.β., with a modification of the spelling of *giltles*, which is usually a trisyllable (see L.G.W. 1982, and *Cant. T.* A. 1312, etc., etc.).

2094 G.R.*A.* It nys (R.A. is) no profre as onto (A *to* for *on-to*) youre kynrede.
F. Hyt is not profet as vnto your kynrede.

β.γ. *profre*; B.T.Th. *profit.* The context requires the former.

In view of this examination, it may be doubted if the F. readings in 1386, 1448, 1472, 2073, 2092, 2094 can be credited to Chaucer. In some of the remaining cases, we may prefer the G. reading to the F. reading, or *vice versa*, but it cannot be said that the variations afford any evidence of revision or emendation one way or the other. It must be added that the presumption must be against the reading of F., when it is opposed to a reading presented by G., R., and A. in common.

F.—G.R.—G.A.—R.A.

I now compare the unique readings of F. with the readings of G.R., G.A., R.A., and, in some cases, the corresponding readings of A., R., and G., respectively. Obviously defective readings of F., of which there are many, are omitted.

670	G.*A.* is	*R.*	F. nys
750	G. that; that	R.A. that; the	F. the; the
			(*N.B.* T.B.=R.A.)
765	G.A. thour thyn lym and thour thyn ston	*R.*	F. thurgh thy lyme and ek thy stoon (*or* for *our*)
805	G.A. there	*R.* tho	F. than
1002	G.A. for	*R.*	F. by
			(*N.B.* T.B.=G.A.)
1053	G.A. to beyseke	*R.*	F. hir beseke
1094	G. Sche manye a beste to the shippis sente	R.A. Ful many a best she to hys shyppes sent	F. Ful many a beeste she to the shippes sent
1217	G. These bestys wilde	*R.*A. These wilde (R. wyld) bestis	F. The wilde hertes
1251	*G.* of a notherys wo	*R.*A. at one otheris (R. anothers) wo	F. at another wo (*N.B.* B.=R.A.)
1255	G.R. of; of; of	A. of; of; and	F. of; and; and (*N.B.* T.B.=A.)
1273	G.A. Not I not (nat)	*R.*	F. Wot I not (*N.B.* T.=G.A.)
1296	G.A. in myn slep (A. slepe) so sore me	*R.*	F. in my slepe me so sore

1345	G.R. So gret a reuthe I haue for tendyte (R. to endyte)	A. so grete a reuth I haue it to endyte	F. so grete routhe I haue hit for to endite (*N.B.* B. om. 1345)
1370	G. tendere; gentil	R.A. gentyl; tendre	F. gentil; gentill
1419	G. Here as; may	R.A. There as; myght (R. om. *this*)	F. There as; may
1559	G.R. somme (R. om. *this*)	A. text	F. sothe
1573	G.	R.A. Myght fynde hym vntrew to hyr also	F. Most fynden him to hir vntrewe alsoo (*N.B.* T. om. *to hir*)
1597	G. doth; was	R.A. dyd; was	F. dothe; is
1647	G.A. stynted, styntet	R.	F. stynten
1753	G. ffor he woste wel she wolde	R.A. for well thought he she wolde	F. For well thoghte he she shulde
1764	G.A. now I-take	R.	F. new y-take
1801	G.R. Wel wot (R. wote) men that a woman hath	A. Wele wote men that wommen haue	F. Wel wote men a woman hath
1835	G.A. forth ne myght she brynge	R. as in G.A. with *may* for *myght*	F. ne may she forthe out brynge

(*N.B. Lines* 1836–1907 *are wanting in* G.)

1839		R.A. tellen were an inpossible	F. telle hyt were impossible (*N.B.* T. om. *hyt*)
1857		R.A. she hede toke	F. hede she toke
1886		R.A. Crete	F. Grece
1888		R.A. Nat for thy sake only wryte I	F. Nat oonly for thy sake writen ys
1940	G.R. and makyn hem	A. and makith thame	F. To make(n) hem (*N.B.* T. conf. G.)
2032	G.R. I wil (var. sp.)	A. wole I	F. I wolde
2046	G.A. me so	R.	F. so me (*N.B.* T.=G.A.)
2084	G. Grace of slyghte and herte	R.A. Grace of hert and sleyght	F. Grace and sleyght of hert
2199	G.A. Hadde (had) he not synne that hire	R.	F. Hath he not synne that he hir (*N.B.* B. om. second *he*)
2226	G.R. this false louere	A. wanting	F. these false lovers
2239	G.A. his	R.	F. this
2255	G.A. ek	R.	F. ful
2286	G.R. that she lovith	A. that sche loued	F. that hir longeth
2291	G.A. beute	R. wanting	F. *bounde* for *bounte* (*N.B.* T.=G.R.)
2443	G.R. hadde (R. had) be	A. had y-be	F. hath y-be (T. *hath be*)
2452	G.A. Philes (Phillis)	R.	F. quene
2477	G.A. he wolde ageyn	R.	F. ageyn he wolde
2503	G.R. mone wente onys	A.	F. mone ones went
2507	*wanting in* G.	R.A. yef	F. yet

2511	G.R. As I or as a trewe louere	A.	F. As I or other trewe lovers (N.B. T. om. *other*)
2534	G. That it mot be	R.A. That hyt may be	F. That hyt be now

(*N.B. Lines* 2551–2616 *are missing in* A.)

2583	G.R. As to these wemen		F. And to this woman
2592	G.R. That what with Venus and othir oppressioun		F. and with Wenus and other oppressyon
2596	G.R. gan to turne		F. gan thoo turne
2603	G.R. lykede; make a maryage		F. lyketh; maken mariage (T.B. make)
2648	G.R. aspis	A.	F. aspe
2686	G.A. in this awer	R.	F. in swich a were

There are small variations in reading in 670, 750, 765, 805, 1002, 1251, 1255, 1273, 1419, 1559, 1597, 1764, 1940, 2032, 2226, 2239, 2255, 2443, 2452, 2507, 2511, 2596, 2603, 2648. The readings of F. should, perhaps, be rejected in all those lines in which one or both of its congeners (T.B.) are in agreement with the other MSS. under consideration. This is found to be the case in 750 (T.B. = R.A.), 1002 (T.B. = G.A.), 1251 (B. = R.A.), 1255 (T.B. = A.), 1273 (T. = G.A.), 1940 (T. = G.R.). Further, the readings of F.—from considerations of grammar or sense— appear to be unsound in 2032, 2507. On the other hand, F. appears to offer the correct reading in 670, 1419, 1753, 2648, 2686.

As regards transposition of words, Chaucer cannot be held responsible for the F. readings in 1296, 1857, 2046, 2477. On the other hand, F. seems to give the correct reading in 2503, as *ones* occupies an almost impossible position in the reading of G.R.

The remaining readings will be considered in detail:—

1053 There is little to choose between the readings of G.A. and F., but the former is perhaps the right one, being found in G.A.γ. The construction of *hire* in *of hire socour to beseke* was apparently misunderstood, for there seems to have been some variety of editing in the MSS.
1094 The reading of F. is practically the same as that of R.A. I am inclined to think that the line, as it stands in G., was amended by the author ; see p. 38.
1217 F. probably edited, *bestys* being altered to *hertis* in view of 1212.
1345 As it stands, F. seems to be metrically unsound.
1370 The repetition of *gentil* in F. can hardly be what the poet intended.
1559 There is little to choose between G.R. and F.
1573 G. is here defective. Only F. gives a good reading.

1647   Here F. appears to give a better construction, but either reading might stand.
1801   F. is perhaps corrupt; for *wot* is uninflected and monosyllabic in the plural. See *Cant. T.*: *Prol.* 829, and *Sq. T.* 511.
1835   The tautology of *forth out*, and the overweighted fourth and fifth measures in the F. reading, cannot be ascribed to Chaucer. Probably *shame* was not recognised as dissyllabic by the individual responsible for the F. reading.
1839   The R.A. reading here is probably correct. See p. 113.
1886   *Grece* in F. is an error for *Crete*.
1888   G. is wanting; R.A. are confirmed by a.β., but both readings are poor from a rhetorical point of view.
2084   F. here makes little sense with its *sleyght of hert*. Chaucer's meaning seems obvious enough: Adriane prays for the grace or blessing of (1) skill, (2) courage on behalf of Theseus. Either G. or R.A. might be adopted.
2199   F. seems unsound here and, though in agreement with T., is not supported by its congener B.
2286   Here γ.=G.R.; β.=A. The reading of F.T.B.—*that hir longeth*—presents a construction without analogy, and is probably corrupt.
2291   F. *bounde* is for *bounte* in B. On the other hand, T.=G.R., and the reading *beaute* is obviously required by the context.
2534   There is little to choose between the readings of G. and F.
2583   Here γ.=G.R.; β.=F.T.B. The reading (*these wemen*) in G.R. appears to be correct, as the author is apparently referring to the *Werdys* in 2580.
2592   The true reading in this line is difficult to decide upon.

I submit that the F. readings in 1217, 1345, 1370, 1801, 1835, 1886, 2084, 2199, 2286, 2291, 2583, should be rejected as not representing what the poet wrote. In 1053, 1559, 1647, 1888, 2534, 2592, the F. readings may be sound, but it is hardly possible to give them the preference. In 1094, 1573, perhaps only F. presents the right reading.

To sum up the results of the examination of the foregoing unique readings of F., it has been shown:—

(1) that there are not many lines in which F. alone gives a reading which can stand against the reading presented by all three MSS. G.,R.,A., or by two of them;

(2) that in most cases in which F. presents a reading which can stand side by side with that in other MSS., there is little to choose between these readings;

(3) that the unique readings of F. provide no evidence, such as the analysis of the G. readings offered, to show that there was anything of the nature of emendation or revision by the author in one direction or another.

Chaucer's Legend of Good Women

The unique readings of R. and A. will now be examined. Both these MSS. present late copies of the poem, and, as might be expected, offer numerous unique readings. Many of these are utterly corrupt, or exhibit unmistakable signs of having been edited. Others are only slightly differentiated from the readings of the other MSS., these smaller variations being similar in character to those indicated in analysing the unique readings of G. and F. As no useful end would be served by giving complete lists, I offer only a few selected examples of these smaller variations, but include in the following lists the more important variations.

The following lists give a selection of the unique readings of R. as against the corresponding readings of G.F.A., and a selection of the unique readings of A. as against G.F.R. :—

R.—G.F.A.

819	G.F.A. the wympyl gan sche	R. gan she the wympyll
1004	G.F.A. clepid	R. called
1097	G.F.A. alwey with hire	R. with hyr alwey
1122	G.F.A. floreynys	R. floures
1210	G.F.A. all corrupt—*this lady* for *thus lat I*	R. And forth thys nobyll quene thus lat I ryde
1236	G.F.A. wel can pleyne	R. can he pleyne
1249	G.F.A. It is a	R. that hyt ys (*see previous line*)
1271	G.F.A. and fastyn	R. he fasteth
1433	G.F.A. spittyn (G. ins. *other*)	R. shottyn
1470	G.F.A. on ; by	R. by ; of
1544	G.F.A. hym Iason	R. thys Iason
1576	G.F.A. and	R. ffor
1683	G.F.A. seyth	R. telleth
1691	G.F.A. starf at	R. dyed in
2003	G.F.A. also (F. om. *hym*)	R. therto
2021	G.F.A. may he	R. he may
2228	G.F.A. the formys	R. fortunes
2236	G.F.A. that from this (A. the)	R. that all thys (furst)
2548	G.F.A. as	R. and
2620	G.F.A. they dryve	R. was dryuyn
2624	G.F.A. let (F. om. *he*)	R. dyd
2651	G.F.A. after	R. with all

A.—G.F.R.

597	G.F.R. gentyl	A. noble
727	G.F.R. wex ; wex	A. wox ; grewe
797	G.F.R. subtyly (R. wympelyd)	A. secrely
803	G.F.R. made hir (R. om. *so*)	A. hir made
1066	G.F.R. lyk (F. om. *that he*)	A. suich
1072	G.F.R. for (F. om. *he*)	A. and ; *he had* for *hadde he*
1084	G.F.R. in this manere	A. and hir manere

1085	G.*F*.R. Sche to hym spak (F. *corrupt*)	A. To him sche spak
1101	G.F.R. of song and of	A. of songis and
1140	G.F.R. that is the god	A. the god that is
1205	G.F.*R*. turne hym	A. him turne
1211	G.F.R. on ; by hire syde	*A*. in ; hir besyde
1365	G.F.R. blowe (blow) awey	A. blowen quite
1375	G.F.R. and humble	A. and thyne humble
1425	G.F.R. callid	A. cleped
1443	G F.*R*. myghte fallyn	A. mycht befallen
1644	G.F.*R*. doth; goth (R, ins. *sone*)	A. maid ; went
1685	G.*F*.R. preyse ; drawe to (G. ins. *me* ; F. *to* for *and*)	A. haue ; draw in
1767	G.F.R. quappe	A. quake
1772	G.F.R. ffor maugre hir	A. maugre hir hede
1801	G.*F*.R. a woman hath (F. om. *that*)	A. wommen haue
2102	G.F.R. vpon (hypermetrical)	A. on
2138	G.F.R. poynt	A. word
2163	G.F.R. amyd the wylde se	A. out in the salt(e) see
2253	G.F.R. al night; balkis	A. at nycht ; wallis
2392	G.F.R. al were he now my brothir	A. were he myn owin brothir
2526	G.F.R. faire	A. false
2626	G.F.R. glad (F. loked, G.R. lokyth)	A. blith
2642	G.F.*R*. al (R. om. *him*)	A. us

An inspection of the above lists shows that even among the variations described by comparison as more important, there is little in the way of a material difference in reading. In forming an opinion on the comparative merits of the various readings, the presumption is against the unique reading of such a MS. as R. or as A., when it is confronted with a reading in which older MSS., such as G. and F., agree.

Only in line 1210 does R. offer a good reading in place of an unsound or defective one in G.F.A.

A. offers a better reading than G.F.R. in 2102, and Prof. Skeat adopts its reading in 1375. In the latter case, it may be doubted if the reading is sound, as it requires the accent to be placed on the second syllable of *obeysaunce*, a word which is generally accented on the first and third syllables (see *L.G.W.* 149, 1268, 2479, and *Cant. T.: Cl.T.* 174).

The following list gives the more important variations when R. is unique and two other MSS. agree :—

Chaucer's Legend of Good Women

R.—G.F.—F.A.

747	G.F. whil that they stode (F. stoden)	A.	R. whyle they stodyn
777	G.F. after come	A. after him	R. aftyrward
815	G. glad that that	F.A. glad that	R. glad of that
837	G. as in this cas	F.A. in this caas	R. in sory cas
1010	G.F. gentillesse; of beute	A. gentinesse; and beautee	R. gentilnes; of beaute
1055	G. whan that; hadden	F.A. whan; had	R. when; haddyn
1099	G. neuere at ese was betyr in al	F.A. neuer better at ese was	R. neuer better at ese was in
1366	G.F. but who so wele al	A. bot quhoso wole	R. but who that wyll
1475	G. were thidyr blowe	F.A. thider were y-blow	R. thedyr were blow
1716	G.F. and ful priuyly into	A. and ful priuely in	R. and pryuyly in to
1743	G.F. blysful (G. 1741)	A. humble	R. blythefull
2396	G. if that like yow	F.A. if that hyt liketh yow	R. yef that hyt lyke yow
2597	G.F. To badde aspectys	A. wanting	R. Ryght bad aspectes

The following list gives the more important variations when A. is unique and two other MSS. are in agreement:—

A.—G.F.—G.R.—F.R.

758	G.F. Why nylt thow cleue or fallyn al a-two	R.	A. Quhy nyltow fall adoun and cleve atwo
777	G.F. after come	R. aftyrward	A. after him
866	G.F. was (F. om. *and*)	R.	A. wox
1010	G.F. gentillesse; of beute	R. gentilnes; of beaute	A. gentilnesse; and beautee
1119	G. shynede be nyghte	F.R. shyneth by nyghte	A. shyneth by the nycht
1259	G. alle how that ye	F.R. al (alle) how they	A. all how that thei
1263	G. as ye may it rede	F.R. as ye may rede	A. as I may rede
1345	G.R. for tendite (to endyte)	F. hit for to endite	A. it to endyte
1352	G. But yit as myn autour right thus sche seyde	F.R. But as myn auctour seythe yit thus she seyde	A. But as myn auctour seith rycht thus sche seid
1353	G.F. Or she was hurt by-forn (F. beforne) or she deyede	R. When she was hurt beforn er that she deyde	A. Quhan she was hurt before that she deid
1360	G.R. contrarye	F.	A. contrair
1366	G.F. but who so wele al	R. but who that wyll	A. bot quhoso wole
1449	G. (om. *and*)	F.R. (om. *that*)	A. And chese quhat folk that thou wilt with the take
1559	G.R. somme (R. om. *this*)	F. sothe	A. text
1743	G.F. blysful	R. blythefull	A. humble

1927	G.R.	F. as ye shal after here	A. rycht thus as ye schall here
1964	G. Thesius	F.R. Mynos	A. king Mynos
1999	G. hath bothe roum and space	F.R. hath roome and eke space	A. and hath roum eke and space
2068	G.F. of traytour	R.	A. of a traytour
2094	G.R. nys (R. ys) no profre as on to	F. is not profet as vnto	A. is no proffer as to
2327	G.F. and that a ryght	R.	A. and that vnrycht
2395	G. o wekid	F.R. of a wikked	A. of euill
2655	G.F.	R.	A. Hide this quod he so that it be nocht sene

(*a*) R. offers what seem to be sound or superior readings in 1055 (also γ.), 1099 (confirmed by P.γ.Rl.), 1716 (confirmed by α., which reads *vn* for *in to*), 2396 (supported by the imperfect line in G.). In 815 (unsupported), 1366 (also in α.), R. seems to be sound in metre, but the readings are open to doubt. In 747 (also α.), 777 (also α.P.), 837 (also α.), 1010, 1475 (unsupported), 1743, 2597 (unsupported), we may suspect corruption.

(*b*) A. offers what seem to be sound or superior readings in 1259 (unsupported), 1353 (also α.), 1360 (unsupported), 1449 (A. avoids the monosyllabic first measure in G., and is unique), 2068 (unsupported).

It presents fair readings in 1263 (*I* for *ye* in α.P.Rl.), 1345 (unsupported), 1352 (unsupported), 1366 (unsupported), 1927 (unsupported), 1964 (unsupported), 1999 (supported by β.), 2094 (unsupported—avoids an extra syllable before the pause), 2655 (unsupported), but in most of these lines the correct reading is a matter of doubt. In 758 (unsupported), 777 (also B.), 866 (*wox* also B.), 1010, 1119 (unsupported), 1559 (unsupported), 1743 (also β.), 2327 (unsupported), 2395 (unsupported), we may suspect editing.

It is possible that R. and A., though evidently later transcriptions than G. or F., have preserved the correct readings in some of the examples indicated above. Unfortunately, several of the readings receive no support from any one of the extant MSS. of the legend. There is no evidence in the lists to justify the suspicion that either R. or A. embodies a recension differing in any material respect from the recension embodied in F.

G.—F.—R.—A.

There now remain for examination the lines in which the MSS. all differ. In numerous cases, the differences are without doubt due to corruption, and, as it would serve no useful purpose fully to detail all these, I propose to classify the instances into three groups:—

(1) lines in which the different readings do not suggest the existence of more than one original, but probably represent a differentiation or a decay from a single original;

(2) lines in which the different readings suggest the existence of more than one original;

(3) lines in which the true reading is doubtful.

N.B. Lines in which there are only very small differences in the readings, such as the omission of *e* final or medial, of *n* in the inflexion of verbs, and obvious errors of scribes, have not been included.

(1) Lines in which the different readings point to the existence of a single original:—

853	original as in G.		trisyllable, as in the *Knightes Tale*)
1063	G.		
1143	F.	1951	G.
1155	G.	1967	R. (*but* for *not*)
1179	G.	1995	G.
1210	R.	2007	G. (*what* for *whan*)
1246	F.	2051	G.
1378	F. (G. sworist)	2075	G.
1489	A. (*schuld* for *schulde*)	2202	F.
1540	F.	2291	G.
1564	G.	2308	G.
1607	F. or R. (*pleuer* for *plener*)	2314	F.
1613	G. (selfe put *or* selfe I-put)	2328	G. (F. *longe*; T. *loude*)
1642	G.	2356	G.
1649	A. (resembles G.)	2369	G.
1751	G.	2393	G.
1785	A. (swerde y-drawe? see T.)	2483	G.
1824	R.	2496	G.
1826	G.	2535	G. (*the* is correct; see 2536, 2538)
1841	F. (*had* for *hadde*, as in T.)		
1847	R.	2579	F.
1863	F. (Tarquyny; see T.)	2593	F.
1875	F.	2637	G.
1881	R.	2667	G.
1892	F.	2676	G. (?)
1897	F. or R. (*Athenes* may be either a dissyllable or	2712	R.
		2714	G. (*forth* in error for *fer*)

It is worthy of remark that, for the last three legends (496 lines), the number of examples (17) in which all four MSS. differ from one another is out of all proportion to the number (33) for the previous legends (1648 lines). A plausible explanation for this is perhaps to be found in the increasing weariness of scribes towards the close of a heavy task, the evil results of which would of course be multiplied by successive transcriptions. On the other hand, it is also worthy of remark that in the first legend, that of Cleopatra, there seem to be proportionately fewer variations than in any succeeding legend.

(2) Lines in which the readings suggest the existence of more than one original :—

730 G. myghte nat; F. wold yt nat; R. wold nat; A. wold it nocht,
    (Perhaps correct reading *nolde nat*).
784 G. metynge *wolde* be; F. metynges *sholde* be; R.A. metyng *shuld* be.
1139 G. But natheles oure autour tellith vs.

F.R.A. each has its own spurious line in place of this. Possibly it was the author's intention to cancel it.

1166 G. Sche waylith and sche makith manye a breyde.
     F. She waketh walwithe maketh many a brayde.
     R. She waketh and waleweth and maketh many abrayde.
     A. She wailith walowith and makith many a breid.

F.R.A. seem to point to a similar origin, different from G.

1173 G. Me thynkith that he is so wel I-wrought.
     F. For that me thinketh he is so wel y-wroghte.
     R. ffor me thynketh he ys so well y-wrought.
     A. For that me think he is so wele ywrocht.

F.R.A. point to a similar origin, different from G.

1203 G. That helith *syke men of* nyghtis sorwe.
     F. *seke folkes of*; R. *folkes of hyr*; A. *seke folk of*.

Here G., F.A., R. show three distinct readings.

1529 G. Of these thre poyntis there nas no man hym liche.
     F. Of these thre poyntes ther nas noon hym liche.
     R. Of these iii poyntes ther was no man hym lyche.
     A. Off thir (for *these*) thre poyntis ther is non him liche.

1727–1730
     G. Myn husbonde is so longe out of this toun
        ffor which the drede doth me so sore smerte
        That with a swerd me thynkyth that to myn herte
        It styngith me whan I thynke on that place.
     F. Myn housbonde ys to longe out of this tovne
        For which the drede doth me so to smerte
        Ryght as a swerde hyt styngeth to myn herte
        Whan I thinke on these (for *the sege*) or of that place.

Chaucer's Legend of Good Women

In 1727 R.A.=F., except that R. reads *the* for *this*.
In 1728 A.=F.; R. ffor whyche the drede of deth doth me to smert.
In 1729 A. (*that* for *ryght*) confirms F.; R. That ys a swerde hyt styngeth me to the hert.
In 1730 R.A. When I thynke of (A. on) the sege or of (A. on) that place.

Here the readings point to two different originals, one represented in G. and the other in F.R.A.

In respect to 1166, 1173, 1203, 1529, 1727–1730, the nature of the variations points to amendment of the text as found in G.

(3) Lines with doubtful readings. These will here be merely indicated by their number, but some of them will be discussed in the appendix to this dissertation :—

639	1046	1353	1721	2215
641	1091	1366	1755	2487
825	1133	1499	1803	2509
903	1338	1538	1837	2671
907	1339	1671	1936	

The various readings of these MSS., when they arranged themselves in pairs (G.F.—R.A., G.R.—F.A., G.A.—F.R.), have also been examined, in view to ascertaining such minor or partial relations as may exist between them.

G.F.—R.A.

The variations between G.F. on the one side and R.A. on the other may be thus classified : (1) readings in R.A. which may be regarded as corrupt or the result of editing ; (2) variations which are *prima facie* of an unimportant character, (3) readings in which R. and A. seem to be sound and G.F. unsound.

(1) Readings in R.A. which may be regarded as corrupt or the result of editing :—

610	*gentylnes* for *gentillesse*		911	*in* for *and*
615	*hyr, hym,* for *hym, hire*		989	R.A. om. *ne*
616	*fest for* for *feste*		1010	*gentilnes* for *gentillesse*
629	*wold* for *wol*		1031	R.A. om. *and*
666	*sweren falsly* for *falsly swere(n)*		1062	*ofter* for *ofte*
			1080	*gentilnes* for *gentillesse*
744	*they* for *ye*		1113	*hym* for *hem*
775	*swete* for *wete*		1141	R.A. om. *hye*
842	*ys* for *be*		1252	*how* for *now*
865	*quake* for *quappe*		1338	R.A. om. *swete*
868	*hert so dere* for *herte deere*		1400	*Eson* for *Pelleus*
873	*wepeth* for *wep*		1447	R.A. ins. *the* unnecess.
910	*but yef* for *but*		1457	*go rede* for *rede*

1491	R.A. ins. *full* unnecess.	2121	*ye haue* for *haue ye*
1495	*play vs* for *pleye*	2209	*had* for *hath*
1506	*they* for *it*	2363	*had* for *hath*
1520	R.A. ins. *that* unnecess.	2441	R.A. dyd him gret honour
1564	R.A. ins *in* unnecess.		G.F. dedyn (F. dede) hym
1610	*was* for *wex*		honour
1674	*thought* for *youthe*	2522	*on* for *of*
1799	R.A. ins. *hir* unnecess.		

(2) Variations which are *prima facie* of an unimportant character :—

680	*the* for *that*	1476	*hym* for *hem*
700	*receuyd* for *receyuyth*	1539	*my* for *and*
770	*euyn* for *eue*	1834	*sat* for *sit*
968	*hyr, thair,* for *hise*	1981	*this* for *his*
1065	*shuld* for *shal*	2179	*more speke* for *more to speke*
1094	*his* for *the*	2279	*the* for *this*
1147	*the* for *this*	2426	*a* for *the*
1403	*the* for *that*	2633	*say* for *seyth*

(3) Readings in which R.A. appear to be superior to G.F. :—

611   R.A. And of dyscrecion and hardynes.
     G.F. And of discrecioun and of hardynesse.
659   R.A. My worshyp in thys world thus haue I lorn.
     G.F. *day* for *world*, perhaps caught from the preceding line.
1215 R.A. That I myght ones mete hym with thys spere.
     G.F. That I myghte hym onys mete with this spere.
1696, 1697   R.A. wrought(e), thought(e); G.F. wroughten, thoughten.

With regard to the variations under the second head, the presumption is in favour of the G.F. and against the R.A. readings, as the former are undoubtedly older transcriptions, while the latter exhibit later and more corrupted texts.

There are two matters of some interest that call for attention in the above analysis: (1) the fact that R. and A. resemble one another so frequently in lines that have been corrupted; (2) the fact that these resemblances, while fairly numerous in legends I.—IV., are few and far between in the remaining legends. This subject will be discussed more fully at a later stage of this dissertation.

The following lists exhibit the readings of G.R. as against those of F.A., and of G.A. against those of F.R. :—

G.R.—F.A.

647	G.R. hem (T.=G.R.)	F.A. him
810	*G.R.* dredy, dredeful	F.A. drery
952	G.R. wolde his	F.A. wolde (A. towardis, wold*e*)
1028	G.R. so wyde	*F.A.* om. *so*
1107	*G.R.* ornementis	F.A. pavements

Chaucer's Legend of Good Women

1254	G.R. wemen (R. *of* for *o*)	F.A. woman
1255	G.R. of, of, of	F. of, and, and (T.B.A. of, of, and)
1392	G.R. al haue he	F.A. all though (alle-thof) he haue
1409	G.R. hadde, had	F.A. hath
1547	G.R. assent	F.A. entent
1605	G.R. as a leoun	F.A. as lyon
1637	G.R. terme set	F.A. terme yset (F. y-sette)
1642	G.R. sauyth (R. thys)	F.A. saved (F.B. there; T. here)
1663	G.R. receyuyth (R. ins *fayre*)	F.A. receyved
1710	G.R. to nyght to Rome	F.A. to Rome to nyght
1795	G.R. upon	F.A. vnto (F. *swerde* for *poynt*)
2112	G.R. wolde (R. wold)	F.A. nolde (A. nold*e*)
2186	G.R. graspith	F. gropeth; A. grapid
2242	G.R. wele, wyll	F.A. wolde (F. om. *it*)
2277	G.R. hyre wele bothe come	F.A. hyr I wil bothe come
2282	G.R. louyth	F.A. loued
2332	G.R. ffor fere (R. *corrupt*)	F. For ferde; A. For fered
2370	G.R. wolde, wold (R. ins. *that*)	F.A. shulde (A. ins. *that*)
2396	G.R. lyke	F.A. liketh
2501	G.R. youre (G. *that* for *which*)	F.A. oure
2519	G.R. is	F.A. nys (F. *the* for *thy*)
2718	G.R. to takyn (take)	F.A. and taken

G.A.—F.R.

864	G.A. therwith	F.R. therwithal
898	G.A. departe now	F.R. now departe (depart)
901	G.A. whilom were(n)	F.R. weren whilom
916	G.A. is (A. piramus and Tisbe)	F.R. are (ar)
1061	G.A. saugh that	F.R. om. *that*
1129	G.A. unto (G. hadde; A. hath)	F.R. to
1144	G.A. as of	F.R. om. *as*
1182	G.A. coude	F.R. couth*e*
1285	G.A. so	F.R. thus (R. depe swore)
1413	G.A. myghte (mycht)	F.R. may
1488	G.A. lodman, ladman	F.R. lodesmen, lodesman
1563	G. hym (for *hem*); A. thame	F.R. hir
1596	G.A. assentede	F.R. assentith
1612	G.A. of whiche	F.R. the whiche
1658	G.A. betraysede	F.R. betrayed (R. ins. *he*)
1779	G.A. hire (A. *sight* for *light*)	F.R. hys
2063	G.A. so yeue; swich a (G. *yow* for *me*)	F.R. to yeve; suche
2115	G.A. haue I-louyd	F.R. haue loved
2164	G.A. dwellede, duelt	F.R. dwelleth
2272	G.A. lawe gan he preye	F.R. lawe and gan hym prey
2517	G.A. She wel hath (G. om. *that*)	F.R. She hath wel

N.B. Lines 1836–1907 *are wanting in G.*
N.B. Lines 2551–2616 *are wanting in A.*

An examination of the above readings shows that the correct or better reading is more generally found in G. than in F., R. or A.

Further, while there is no indication of any special relation between G. and R., or G. and A., or F. and R., there are three remarkable examples of agreement between F. and A. in 1107 (*pavements* for *ornementis*), 1547 (*entent* for *assent*), 2277 (*myself with hyr I wil* for *myn self with hyre wele*). In these lines the readings of F. and A. are apparently corrupt, and, as it is hardly possible to regard resemblances in such corruptions as a result of accident, we are perhaps justified in suspecting the existence of some special relationship between the text of F. and that of A.

Summary of the Results of the Collation of G.F.R.A.

I now summarise the deductions that may be made from the foregoing investigation :—

MS. G.g. 4. 27. *Camb. Univ.*—This MS. presents a large number of unique readings which distinguish it as clearly from R. and A. as from F.; consequently, it would not be consistent with the facts of the case to describe R. and A. as presenting texts of the same type as G.

As several of the unique readings of G., which appear to be quite sound in themselves, stand against apparently superior readings presented by F.R.A. in common, or by two of these, we may conclude that G. represents an earlier draft of the legends, and that F.R.A. represent a revised draft or revised drafts of the legends. This important conclusion will presently receive fuller treatment, and the revised and unrevised lines will be placed in juxtaposition in a special list.

There is no satisfactory evidence of revision after the legend of Ariadne. See pp. 42-44.

Except in respect to the lines above referred to, G. stands out prominently among the four MSS. as the best authority for the text of the legends.

Fairfax MS. 16, *Bod. Lib.*—This MS. presents a large number of unique readings which distinguish it from G.,R.,A. Many of these unique readings seem to be corruptions, and, in other cases, there is not much to choose between the readings of F. and the other MSS. collated with it.

F. embodies the improved or revised readings above referred to, but the evidence provided by its unique readings is insufficient to justify a suspicion that it may represent a revision later than that which is found in R. and A. In a few instances, its readings may perhaps be preferred to the corresponding readings in the other MSS., and possibly embody some of the author's emendations that have not found their way into R. or A.

MS. R. 3. 19. *Trin. Coll., Camb.*; *MS. Arch. Seld.*, B. 24, *Bod. Lib.*—Both of these MS. are distinguished from G. by presenting most of the improved or revised lines.

Each MS. presents numerous unique readings, but neither offers any evidence to justify a suspicion that it presents a later revision than that which is found in F. Moreover, the unique readings, with few exceptions, must be regarded as corruptions.

One or the other is, or both of them are, in agreement with G. in the large majority of the lines in which F. shows peculiar readings. Again, when R. or A. presents readings which are different from the readings presented in common by G. and F., the former in most cases seem to be corrupt. It follows that the texts in R. and A. must be held to occupy positions intermediate between the text in G. and that in F.

Inasmuch as these MSS. are frequently in agreement with G. when it differs from F., or with F. when it differs from G., and as the differences between R. and A., though numerous, are, for the most part, evidently the results of corruption, we may regard R. and A. as presenting nearly the same type of text. They are possibly descended from the same first-hand copy of the poem, or two duplicate first-hand copies.

Further, it has been shown that R. and A. frequently agree in readings which are different from those presented by G.,F. in common, or by each separately. The explanation of these many resemblances may perhaps be found in the hypothesis that both MSS. are descended from a corrupt and not very remote ancestor, or in the hypothesis that at some stage of transcription a scribe responsible for the text in one of these MSS. borrowed some of his readings from the other MS. or some text of the same type. The problem of the relations between R. and A. is complicated by two considerations: (1) that the special resemblances between R. and A. now under reference are few in number in the later legends; (2) that there are signs of some relationship between A. and a MS. of the F. type. The subject of the relations between R. and A. will be discussed in some detail in the article dealing with A.

Section ii.—Revision of the Legends.

The various lists given on pp. 8, 12, 28, indicating the lines which, it is suggested, may have undergone revision, are here consolidated into a single list:—

718	1094	1191	1734
730	1099	1203	1753
780	1112	1212	1788
784	1115	1267	1922
798	1135	1283	1923
856	1160	1529	1933
887	1166	1702	1948
928	1170	1727	1978
932	1171	1728	1984
944	1173	1729	2009
960	1175	1730	2188
961	1187		

The question whether or no there was a revision of the legends is of considerable importance, and merits full investigation. It has been shown that G. offers the least corrupted text of the legends, and is the best authority for the text, and that, nevertheless, in several lines in which its readings appear to be in accordance with what is generally accepted as Chaucer's method in respect to language and metre, the corresponding readings in the other MSS. present what appear to be obvious improvements. This paradox appears to find its only legitimate explanation in the hypothesis that the text, as we find it in G., underwent revision at the hands of the author himself.

Whether the so-called revised lines really involve improvements can be decided only by an examination in detail of the lines in question, but, before attempting this examination, I would anticipate certain objections that may possibly be urged against the acceptance of the theory of revision.

In the first place, it may be suggested that I have referred only to lines which point to a revision of the text as found in G., and that I have ignored lines which may point to a revision of the text in the opposite direction. Such an objection, if it could be substantiated, would certainly invalidate the hypothesis. But I submit it cannot be substantiated. The lists prepared by me are, to the best of my belief, approximately exhaustive in character, as, being desirous of arriving at the truth, I have endeavoured to state the case with fairness. It is true that numerous examples in which G. gives the

Chaucer's Legend of Good Women

better reading can be, as they have been, cited, but an examination of these will show that, in almost every instance, the text in the other MSS is corrupt, or, in other words, that the difference between the readings is not the difference between one good reading and another good reading, but the difference between a good reading and one that betrays signs of unsoundness.

In the second place, it may be urged that the lines in G. under consideration are themselves, perhaps, examples of corruption as a result of "editing" by some individual or individuals responsible for the text in its present form, and that if, instead of standing in solitary grandeur, G. could be collated with and checked by the readings of some MS. between which and G. subsisted relations as close as those subsisting between F. and T. and B., or between R. and a., or between A. and β., the hypothesis that G. presents an earlier draft of the legends could not be maintained. Now, one of the propositions implied in this objection involves a contradiction in terms. If such a congener could be discovered, its collation with G., without doubt, would indicate places in which G. has been corrupted, but if it did not confirm several of the readings under reference, it would have as little claim to be regarded a congener as either R. or A. The objection implies a second proposition—that it is possible to regard the readings of G. under reference as the work of some individual other than the poet himself. An investigation of the transcriptions of Chaucer's poems makes it evident that scribes or editors allowed themselves considerable licence in manipulating texts, and were frequently unrestrained by any diffidence in the matter of bringing the text into harmony with their own ideas of propriety in respect to language and metre. Possibly, in a few of the lines indicated,* it might be held that the G. readings are the result of accident, or are due to the idiosyncrasies of some self-constituted editor, but I cannot believe that the student of Chaucer exists who would refuse to see Chaucer's hand in the majority of these readings. The simple fact that, on comparison of two readings, one of them seems to be superior, is not enough to condemn the other, which in itself may be good.

Thirdly, it may be urged that the *improvements* which, it is

* See 784 (*wolde* for *shulde*), 1187 (*thing* for *wyght*), 1191 (*wolde* for *wol*), 1267 (*trewe* for *privy*), 1367 (*rede he* for *rede*), 1753 (*he woste wel* for *wel thoughte he*), 1788 (*quod she is that* for *ys that quod she that*), 1978 (*leue systyr Phedra dere* for *Phedra leue suster dere*).

suggested, exist in F.R.A. may be due to *editing*. Possibly, in some of the lines indicated, the variations may be ascribed to a self-constituted editor, but, if all the examples given be examined with care, it is hardly possible to credit all the *improvements* to an editor, unless the poet himself had been acting in this capacity. Moreover, it will be seen on examination that the differences between the readings of G. and of the other authorities in the case of the legends are, in many instances, of the same nature as the differences in the readings of the two Prologues: see Part II. sect. i.

I now proceed to quote the various readings under discussion, which, individually in several instances, and also cumulatively, appear to carry with them a justification of the hypothesis that the legends—or some of them—underwent revision. A comparison of the different readings may afford us some insight into Chaucer's method of work and principles of versification.

A comparison of readings in lines which appear to have undergone revision.

N.B. To save space, when two or more MSS. are in practical agreement, the line is quoted as it stands in one of them—generally the first mentioned.

718 G. That tho was in that lond Estward dwellynge.
F.R. That esteward in the worlde was tho dwellynge.

A. *aftirward, this,* for *esteward, the,* but otherwise confirms F.R.; T.B.Th.a. (*non* for *tho*) Ff. confirm F.R. It follows that G. is unique. Its reading cannot be regarded as involving a mere error of transposition: though sound in sense and metre, it is obviously inferior in rhythm.

780 G. And to begile here wardeynys echon.
F.R.A. And to begile hire (R. theyr; A. thaire) wardeyns euerychone.

Here T.B. (*wardeynes*) Th.a.Ff. confirm F.R.A.; P. is corrupt, but reads *euerychon*. If G. is not corrupt, the change points to a distaste for an accented inflexion. But see lines 283, 484 in F.

796–799 G. . . . sche stal a wey ful pryuyly
    . . . .
    And alle hire frendis for to saue hire trouthe
    Sche hath forsake . . .

F. . . . she stale a-wey ful prevely
    . . . . . .
    For al hire frendes for to saue hire trouthe
    She hath for-sake. . . .

T.B.Th.R.A. agree with F.; *a. ffro* for *For*; P.Rl. begin the line with "alle." The change indicates a preference for *hypotaxis*.

  856 G. Be comyn hidir and may me nat I-fynde (also Th.)
         F.A. Be comen hider and may me nat fynde.

T.B. (*come*), R. (*com*), *a.* (*come*), P.γ.Ff. confirm F.A. It might be urged that the reading *I-fynde* in G. is a copyist's error, but it is remarkable that G. frequently omits the verbal prefix (*I* or *y*), where many of the other MSS. insert it (see 938 G. *lowe brought*, F. *lowe y-broghte*; 963 G. *hadde take*, F. *had y-take*; 1637 G. *terme set*, F. *terme y-sette*). The change in the line brings the necessary rhetorical emphasis on *me*, and also eliminates an extra syllable ending in a consonant at the cesural pause. See 944, 1283, 1529, 1702, 2188 below.

  887 G. Tysbe ryst vp with-outyn ony bost.
         F.*A.* Tesbe rist vppe withouten (A. without) noyse or booste.

R. is corrupt, but confirms F.A., as do T.B.Th.*a.* (ins. *this* before *Thisbe*) P. (*aryseth*) γ.Ff. The reading of G. is sound in sense and metre, but the rhythm of the line is improved by the removal of the recurrent sounds *yn, on* in immediate sequence.

  928 G. In Naso and Eneydos wele I take.
         F.R. In thyne Eneyde and Naso wol I take.

A is corrupt, also Rl.; but T.B.Th.*a.*P.γ. agree with F.R. The change involves a rhetorical improvement by bringing the line into connection with the invocation in the preceding lines.

  932 G. Feynynge the hors I-offerede to Mynerue.
         F.A. Feynyng the hors offered vnto Mynerve.

R.*a.*P. (*to* for *unto*) Rl. read *ffeyned, offred* (v. sp.); T.B.Th.γ. confirm F.A. For the verbal prefix, see remarks on 856 above. The change was presumably due to a desire to get rid of the unpleasant hiatus caused by placing the prefix before a verb beginning with a vowel. I know of no other example of such a use in Chaucer, except perhaps *Rom. Rose*, 1315: *The daunces than y-ended were.*

  944 G. His owene fadyr I-clepid Anchises.
        F.*R.* His olde (R. old) fader cleped Anchises.

A. is corrupt; T.B.Th.*a.*P.γ. confirm F.R. The change removes the extra syllable before the pause as in 856 above.

960, 961   G. With schepis vii and with no more nauye
           And glad was he to londe for to hye.

These two lines occur in P.γ.Rl., but are omitted in F.T.B.Th.R.A.α. The omission may have been the result of accident, but, on the other hand, it should be observed (1) that the omission does not affect the sense or structure of the context; (2) that 960 is a weak line; (3) that such petty details as the number of ships are unnecessary in a story which, as the poet says, is to be confined to essentials. The fact that these lines are omitted in so many of the texts is in favour of the hypothesis that Chaucer cancelled them.

1094   G. Sche manye a beste to the shippis sente.
       F.R.A. Ful many a beeste she to the (R.A. his) shippes sente.

All the authorities agree with or confirm F.R.A. The change removes the harshness of the first measure in G., which is spondaic in character, and involves an improvement in the rhythm of the line.

1099   G. He neuere at ese was betyr in al hese lyve.
       F.A. He neuer better at ease was his lyue.
       R. He neuer better at ease was in hys lyue.

Only B. agrees with F.A., while T.Th.α. (ins. *he* after *was*) P.γ.Rl. confirm R. It is worthy of notice that the scribe of G. has entered a double cesura mark after *neuere*, cesura marks being generally conspicuous by their absence in G., and has erased and corrected part of the line. We may take it that he was particularly careful over this line, and therefore it is not open to us to assume that he was guilty of an error. As a matter of fact, the reading of G. is metrically sound enough, *neuer* being pronounced as a monosyllable before a vowel. The other readings afford a better grammatical collocation of words.

1112   G. ffor hise ese and for to take his reste.
       F.R.A. To take his ease and for to have his reste (R.A. rest).

T.B.Th.α. (*take* for *haue*) P.Rl. (*take* for *haue*) agree with or confirm F.R.A. The change gives a better balance to the construction.

1115   G. Ne stede for to iuste wel to gon.
       F.R. Ne stede for the iustyng wel to goon.

A. like F.R., but inserts *yit* before *stede*; T.B.Th. agree with F.R.; P. *the Iuste*, Rl. *the iustis*. The emendation removes the awkwardness of construction in the succession of infinitives.

1160   G. Now to theffect now comyth the freut of al.
         F.A. Now to theffecte now to the fruyt of al.

T.B.Th.γ. confirm F.A.; the other MSS. are corrupt. The change gives a balance to the construction. See 1112 above.

1166   G. Sche waylith and sche makith manye a breyde.
         F. She waketh walwithe maketh many a brayde.
         R. She waketh and waleweth and maketh many abrayde.
         A. She wailith walowith and makith many a breid.

T. agrees with F.; B. *walith* for *waketh*. The others are corrupt, but confirm F. in its verbs. The reading of F. or of A. is a great improvement on that in G. in the greater descriptive power and the harmonising of sound and sense.

1170–1171   G. Now *leue* sistyr myn what may it be
                 That me agastith in myn *slep* quod she.
              F.R.A. Now *dere* suster myn what may it be
                 That me agasteth in my *dreme* quod she (R. quoth).

T.B. (*quoth* for *quod*) Th.α.P.Rl. agree with or confirm F.R.A. The object of the change here, I suggest, is to get rid of the sibilancy of the second line, and to secure at the end of the sentence an alliterative echo.

1173   G. Me thynkith that he is so wel I-wrought.
         F. For that me thinketh he is so wel y-wroghte.
         A. For that me think he is so wele ywrocht.

R.α. like F., but omit *that*; T.B.Th.P.Rl. agree with F. Here, as also perhaps in 1160, one object of the change appears to be the avoidance of a repetition in immediate sequence of the sound of *th*: see Part II. sect. i. Moreover, hypotaxis replaces parataxis.

1175   G. And ek thereto so mech (e) good he can.
         R.A. And therwith al so (A. as) moche good he can.

F.B.T., *withal* for *ek thereto*; α. (om. *he*) P. agree with R.A. The change is an improvement in sound, and avoids the repetition of *ek*, which occurs in the preceding line.

1203   G. That helith syke men of nyghtis sorwe.
         A.F. That helith seke folk (F. folkes) of nyghtis sorowe.
         R. That heleth folkes of hyr nyghtys sorow.

T.Th. confirm F.; α. agrees with R.; B. = A. In P.Rl. there is another reading resembling R. Either A. or R. is an improvement on G., the consonantal ending of *folk* or *folkes* better defining the close of the verse section at the pause.

1212   G. The hirde of hertis is I-founde anon.
          F.A. The heerde of hertes founden ys anoon.

R.*a*. *byn foundyn* (*ffounde*); T.B.Th.P. confirm F.A.; Rl. *is founden*. The reason for the change seems obvious, removing as it does the unpleasant assonance in the middle of the line in G.

1283   G. Of othere landys than of Cartage quien.
        F.R.A. Of other lande than of Cartage a (A. the) quene.

T.B.Th.*a*.P.Rl. agree with F.R.A. In G. the scansion is obscure. If *Cartage* is a trisyllable, we have what may be an extra syllable ending in a consonant at the cesural pause. For this see above 856, 944. If *Cartage* is a dissyllable, then the vowel in the second syllable of "Cartage" presumably being long, the line would give a somewhat heavy penultimate syllable, which is very uncommon in Chaucer.

1529   G. Of these thre poyntis there nas no man hym liche.
        F. Of these thre poyntes ther nas noon hym liche.

R.*a*. resemble G. with *was* for *nas*; T.B.Th. (*was* for *nas*) γ. (*was* for *nas*) A. (*is* for *nas*) agree with or resemble F. Here the object of the change appears to be the removal of the extra syllable ending in a consonant (see 856, 944, 1283 above).

1702   G. And lat vs speke of weyuys and that is best.
        F.R.A. And let vs speke of wifes that is best.

T.B.Th.*a*. β. (*ar* for *is*) γ. omit second *and*. For the change see 856, 944, 1283, 1529.

1727–1730   G. Myn husbonde is so longe out of this toun
              ffor which the drede doth me so sore smerte
              That with a swerd me thynkyth that to myn herte
              It styngith me whan I thynke on that place.
        F.A. Myn housbonde ys to longe out of this tovne
              For which the drede doth me so to smerte (A. smert)
              Ryght (A. that) as a swerde hyt styngeth to myn herte
              Whan I thenke on the sege (F. *these* for *the sege*) or of
                  (A. on) that place.

T. (ins. *within*; *stinteth* in 1729) B. are in accordance with F., even in respect to the error in the last line quoted. The other MSS. show variations, but, where not corrupt, they are in general agreement with F.A., and confirm the view that lines 1729, 1730 were recast. The sibilancy of the latter part of the second line in G. has been removed in the emendation. The third and fourth lines have been greatly strengthened in sense; the recurrence of the sound

1734   G. And mekely hyre eyen let she falle.
    F.R.A. But mekely (F. mekly) she let hir eyen falle.

All the remaining authorities agree with F.R.A. The reading in G. cannot well be regarded as an error of transposition. The other reading exhibits a marked improvement in rhythm.

1922, 1923   F. Athenes wanne (T. wan) thys kynge Mynos also
    And Alcites (=Alcitoe) and other tovnes mo.

These lines, which, with variations, occur in the other authorities, are not found in G., and the question arises whether they were omitted by the scribe or they were absent from the draft of the poem from which G. was copied. In G. line 1921 (which is practically the same in all the authorities) runs :—

But that tale were to longe as now for me.

After this line G. reads :—

1924   But this theffect that Mynos hath so dreuyn
1925   Hem of Athenys that they mot hym yeuyn
1926   ffrom yer to yer hire owene childeryn dere.

Now it will be seen that, in 1924, G. reads *but* in place of *and* in the other texts, and the line gives the impression that Chaucer wishes to hark back to the main story from which he had commenced to digress in 1902. Minos had started to avenge his son's death at Athens, but Chaucer at this point suddenly digresses into an episode concerning the daughter of Nisus and her relations with Minos at Alcathoe. On revision, I suggest, he observed the hiatus in the narrative, and in order to mark the end of the episode and its connection with the main narrative, interpolated lines 1922, 1923, at the same time changing *but* to *and* in 1924.

1933   G. They caste lot and as it *fil* aboute.
    A. They casten lot and as it *com* aboute.

All the authorities, with slight variations of reading, show *come* for *fil*, and this change gives an alliterative consonantal echo to which Chaucer seems partial.

1948   G. And forth is *gon* this woful yonge knyght.
    F. And forth ys *lad* thys woful yonge knyght.

All the MSS. confirm the substitution of *lad* for *gon*. Not only does this change affect an alliteration on two consonants, *f*, *l*, but it breaks a rather monotonous series of vowel sounds.

1984 G. He shal been holpyn how so euer we do.
   F.R.A. He shal be holpen how soo that we do.

All the authorities agree with F.R.A. If G. be not corrupt, the change points to a preference for a line of ten syllables, for *euer* is generally dissyllabic before a consonant.

2008, 2009 G. . . . he shal *as* (for *at*) hym lepe,
    And slen hym *as* they comyn more to hepe.
   T. . . . he shal *on* hym lepe,
    To slen hym *or* they comen more to hepe.

F. (*the* for *they*, *helpe* for *hepe*) B.Th.R.A.β.γ. (*kepe* for *hepe*) agree with or confirm T., so that G. is unique. The construction is rendered more compact and the sense clearer by the change.

2188 G. I am betrayed and al hire her to-rent.
   F.R.A. I am betrayed (A. betraised) and hir heer to-rent.

T. (*hert* for *heer*) B.Th.β.γ. confirm F.R.A. The change reduces the number of syllables, and gets rid of an extra syllable at the pause.

Besides the above instances there are others which possibly should be included in this list, the changes in the readings being, perhaps, due to the author himself; *e.g.*, 730 (*nolde* for *myghte*), 870 (*Hath Thisbe now* for *Hath Thisbe tho*), 1135 (*presentynge* for *presentis*), 1718 (*they abyde* for *they gan abyde*).

Revision ends with Sixth Legend.

The lists stop short at the legend of Ariadne. The only lines in the three remaining legends which afford ground for a suspicion that there may have also been a revision of the draft of these legends as we find it in G. are 2293, 2294, 2345, 2396, 2539, 2579 (G. *shal*; F.R. *shulde*), 2712 (G. *gret*; F.R.A. *good*). With the exception of 2579, 2712, concerning which discussion would be futile, I shall deal with these *seriatim* :—

2293 G. how so euere he do; F.A. how soo that hyt goo.

All the other authorities agree with or confirm F.A. I can suggest no reason for regarding the alteration as an improvement. It was, I suspect, due to some early editor who did not understand Chaucer's practice of treating *euer* (and similar words) before a vowel or initial *h* as a monosyllable (see Manly: *Observations*, sect. 90, p. 87). *Euer* has been changed to *that* in 1984, but the former word in G. precedes a consonant.

2294   G. and with hise wilis he so fayre hire preyede.
        F.R.A. and with hys wiles kneled and so preyde.

All the authorities agree with or confirm F.R.A. On the face of it G. is corrupt, for Tereus is pleading with Pandion and not with "Philomene," to whom at the time a man so full of *wiles* would not have paid his addresses. The insertion of *hire* in the G. text looks like an *error of the ear*, errors of the ear being not infrequent, though perhaps not so common as errors of the eye. It seems to me that the reading originally may have been *and with his wiles he so fayre preyede*, and that *hire* was, in error, interpolated. If this was the original reading, it is easy to understand how a scribe who did not recognise the dissyllabic value of *fayre* might have made the change indicated in the reading of F.R.A., which was possibly suggested to him by 1232. There is nothing to be said in favour of the second reading.

2345   G. And swor that he say his sistyr ded.
        F.A. And swore hir that he fonde hir suster dede.

Here G. *say* for *fonde* in all the MSS. The G. reading gives an excessive sibilancy, but it is not improbably an error of the scribe, whose weariness of hand or eye, or whose inattentiveness, seems sufficiently attested at this point by the existence of two errors in the line, the omission of *hire* and the substitution of *his* for *hir*.

2396   G. That m(a)y ye wete if that (it) like yow.
        F.A. That may ye fynde yf that hyt lyketh yow.

Here G. *wete* (for *fynde* in all the MSS.) is not improbably an error of the scribe, as the line has been carelessly transcribed. At all events, there is nothing to choose between the readings.

2539   G. That men may rede forby
        F. That folke may reden forth by (R.A. for by) } as they go.

Here all the MSS. confirm F. *Folk* secures the effect of alliteration, but *men* may have been caught from line 2537.

Now, I submit that these examples do not afford evidence that the variations are due to revision by the author. Except perhaps in 2345, there is no ground for expressing a decided preference for the second reading in any instance, and consequently these variations could not well have been included in the above lists.

In view of the absence of evidence of revision in the legends of "Philomene," Phyllis, and Hypermnestra, it is a plausible hypothesis that these legends were written after the revision of the other legends was completed.

There is another circumstance which appears to distinguish these three legends from their predecessors. There are no headings to the legends in α., and there seems to be only one in a contemporary hand in G.;* in F.T.B.β.γ. there are headings in Latin, and in R. and P. there are headings in English. In A. the close of one legend and the beginning of another are, in some cases, indicated at the end of a legend. In the headings of F.T.B., Cleopatra, Thisbe, Dido, Hypsipyle, Medea, Lucrece, are described as *martyrs*. The same term is applied in P. to Dido, Hypsipyle, and Medea; in β. to Lucrece, and Ariadne; and in γ. to Hypsipyle, Medea, Lucrece, and Ariadne. In none of the MSS. is the term applied to "Philomene," Phyllis, or Hypermnestra. If the legends of these three ladies were written after the revision of the prologue and the earlier legends, it is not improbable that there were early MSS. in existence which presented only the revised prologue and *six* legends.

Section iii.—Description of the MSS.

I shall now describe the different authorities for the text of the L.G.W., and endeavour to determine their comparative value and the relationships subsisting between them. In the absence of direct information as to the history of a given Chaucer MS., it is necessary to rely entirely on the internal evidence afforded by its language and versification for the determination of its character and relations. By a comparison of two or more texts in respect to these matters, we may inductively arrive at some knowledge of their comparative value, their relative age, and their mutual relationships. Obviously, however, the method under consideration has its limitations. The internal evidence may be such as to justify an inference that two or more MSS. are descended from a common ancestor, but it may be altogether inconclusive in determining the number of transcriptions

---

* In G. the titles of the legends are given at the foot of a leaf or in the space between the end of one legend and the beginning of another, but the handwriting suggests that these were added at a later date.

which intervened between the common ancestor and each of its descendants. Again, in judging of the relative age of two MSS., differences in their language and versification may justify an inference that one is older than another, but such evidence rarely affords a basis for accurately measuring the difference in time that separates the transcriptions. For instance, there can be no doubt that a considerable number of years separated the transcriptions of G. and R., but it is not possible to specify the number with any approximation to accuracy. Again, when the differences between two MSS. are not very great, it would be dangerous to assume that the copy with the fewest corruptions and bad verses was necessarily the older, for allowance must be made for differences, psychological and sociological, in the characteristics of the scribes responsible for the transcripts. For example, the same MS. might conceivably have been copied by two scribes in the same year—let us say in the third decade of the fifteenth century—and it would not be a matter of wonder if their transcripts differed considerably, as each would have been under the influence of his own distinctive habits of speech; and, as his aim would have been not so much an exact reproduction of his original as a copy intended for the amusement or edification of his readers, it is probable that he would manipulate his text to satisfy his own tastes and standards in respect to grammar, diction, or melody. In these circumstances, great caution is necessary in dealing with views suggested by internal evidence, and I have been careful in the following articles to distinguish hypothesis from demonstration, and have endeavoured to resist the temptation of suggesting views for which adequate support could not be advanced.

Camb. Univ. MS. G.g. 4.27, on parchment, well written.—This MS. contains the unique transcript of what may be legitimately regarded as an earlier form of the Prologue to the L.G.W., and also a copy of each of the completed legends and of the Hypermnestra fragment. Reasons have been given in support of the view that G. presents the text of some of the legends in an earlier and unrevised form.

The Prologue in G. has 545 lines as against 579 in the revised form of it. The scribe would appear to have omitted at least two lines between line 130 and line 131, for the last-mentioned line has no grammatical or logical connexion with any of the preceding lines. Leaf 469 of the MS. has been torn out, involving the loss of lines 1835—1907. Moreover, this MS. omits lines 1922, 1923, 2506, 2507, which are found in other MSS., while it presents two lines, 960, 961, which are found also in P.Rl.γ., but are wanting in the others. G. exhibits another peculiarity in the order of some of its lines: 1738-41 in G. are 1740-3 in the others, while 1742-3 in G. are 1738-9 in the others. It is worthy of remark that neither the omission of the couplets nor the transposition of the lines referred to causes any violation to the sense of the context.

The orthography of the MS. is at first view strange, but appears to be governed by certain principles, though perhaps these are not strictly adhered to. The following features may be noted :—

(1) a single letter is, with few exceptions, employed to represent long as well as short vowels, e.g. *don* (*doon*), *gon* (*goon*), *spak* (*spake*), *fleth* (*fleeth*), etc. ;

(2) *re* is written in place of *r* in the termination of words, eg. *euere*, *louere*, *lengere*;

(3) *y*, sometimes *i*, takes the place of *e* in inflexional terminations closed with a consonant, e.g. *pottyn* (inf.), *boundyn* (past part.), *bokys* (plur.), *stekid* (past part.);

(4) the full form of a verb or of the plural of a noun is generally written, though the vowel of the inflexional termination may be silent, e.g. *louede so* (607), *hadde him* (615), *wolde no* (671), *serpentys* (679);

(5) the forms *myn*, *thyn* are regularly used, whether before vowels or consonants ; *his* before a plural noun is often written *hise* (cf. 882, 885), but this use is uncertain, as the form *hise* occurs before singulars as well ;

(6) *sch* sometimes interchanges with *sh* (*schal, shal*);

(7) *wele* is almost invariably used for *wil, wol*.

Many other peculiarities in the orthography of G. have been pointed out by Dr. Furnivall in his *Temporary Preface* (Chaucer Soc., pp 51–9).

It is hardly necessary to enter here on the grammatical features of the text in this MS., as this subject has been exhaustively treated in the *Observations on the Language of Chaucer's " Legend of Good Women "* by J. M. Manly. This excellent work indirectly demonstrates that the language of the text in G. is that which is accepted by scholars as the language of Chaucer. It is sufficient to state here that, as a rule (to which, without doubt, there are many exceptions), G. exhibits an *e* when sonant as an inflexion or as an integral part of a word. In verbs, nouns, and adjectives, the *e* is generally written where required by grammar and metre, and omitted when not so required; but there are several instances in which the MS. fails in this respect.

Though there are several instances in which the text in G. fails to do justice to Chaucer's grammar and melody, and has to some small extent been edited (see 1178, 1482, 1975), there can be no question that, on the whole, G. offers a better transcript of the legends than any of the other MSS. That it presents an older copy of the poem than F., T., or B. can be shown in many ways, but more particularly by the way in which it distinguishes between the forms of the past tense and past participle of weak verbs,* by its spelling of strong preterites (e.g. G. *wep, tok, spak*, F. *wepe, toke spake*), and by its retention of the final *e* representing an inflexion or otherwise in the rime-words of the couplets.

I quote a few lines from G. and the F.T.B. group in view to illustrating their comparative value :— †

    675   G. And *putte* ful the schryne of spicerye.
             F.B. And *put* ful the shryne of spicerye.

    724   G. This *yonge* man was callyd Piramus.
             F. This *yong* man was cleped Piramus.

    1055   G. And whan that they *hadden told* al here distresse.
             F.T. And whan they *had tolde* al hire distresse.

    1155   G. Entendedyn to spekyn and to *pleye*.
             F.T.B. Entededen for to speke and for (B. om.) to *pley*.

It is admitted that several items may be debited to the other side of the account, but there can be no dispute as to the side on which the balance will be found to stand.

As a result of the investigation, many of the details of which have been embodied in an earlier section of this dissertation, we may hold that G. is without doubt the best authority for the lines which, so far as can be ascertained, do not appear to have undergone modification.

* An exception to this statement must be made in the case of past participles when, instead of the usual *i* or *y* of the inflected part, the scribe employs *e*. The inflexion is then often represented by *ede* (see 151, 157, 159, 164, 242, etc.).

† See also the list of the F.T.B. readings on pp 51–3.

Fairfax MS. 16, *Bod. Lib.*—*Tanner MS.* 346, *Bod. Lib.*—*Bodley MS.* 638, *Bod. Lib.*

These three MSS. may be taken together; for, as will be presently shown, they are all closely related to one another. They present a revised draft of the Prologue, and, as already shown in the case of F., a revised draft of the legends.

F. omits the following lines: 249, 487, parts of 502 and 503, 846, 960, 961, 1490, 1643, 1693, 1998, 2150-53 (in place of which there is a single line compounded of parts of the first and last of these), 2193, 2338 (for which a spurious line is substituted as 2339), 2475. Moreover, the third *strophe* of the *balade* follows line 277. It is characteristic of this MS. that the scribe has marked the pauses in nearly all the lines. However, in some instances the pause marks would appear to have been misplaced.

B. omits lines 157, 249, 487, 846, 960, 961, 1345, 1490, 1643, 1866, 1998,* 2150-53 (in place of which there is a single line compounded of parts of the first and last of these), 2193, 2338 (for which a spurious line is substituted as 2339), 2475. Besides, the order of lines 1776, 1777 is inverted, and the following lines are imperfect owing to injury to the MS.: 1461-63, 1489-95.

T. omits lines 249, 487, 846, 960, 961, 1378-79 (in place of which there is one line compounded of parts of these), 1490, 1643, 1998, 2150-53 (in place of which there is a single line compounded of parts of the first and last of these), 2338 (for which a spurious line is substituted as 2339). Further, the order of lines 2494, 2495 has been inverted.

As regards the orthography of these MSS. there is more or less resemblance. The letter *e* frequently takes the place of *y* or *i* in the inflexional terminations in F. and T., but more rarely in B. F. shows a tendency to double letters in the case of long vowels.

In respect to grammatical forms they are also closely alike, and exhibit unmistakable traces of the decadence of inflexions and an uncertainty as to the grammatical or metrical value of *e* final. In many cases *e* is added when not required for grammar or metre.

To illustrate these statements, I quote a few lines from these MSS.:—

  853-5 F. Now Tesbe which that wyste nat this
      But syttyng in hire drede she thought thus
      Yf so falle that my Piramus.

  * For this a spurious line is substituted in a later hand as 1999.

Chaucer's Legend of Good Women

B. Now Tesbe which that knewe not thys
but syttynge yn her drede she thoght thus
If so fall*e* that my Pyramus.

T. Now Tesbe which þat wist nat this
But sittynge in hir drede she thought thus
If it so fall*e* that my Piramus.

Further examples will be found in the line-to-line analysis given below.

In view of their general resemblance in orthography and grammar, and more especially in the decay of inflexions, there can be little doubt that the three MSS. are approximately of the same age, and are later copies of the poem than G. In 853 (*knewe* for *wiste*), 1591 (*noble* for *maister*), 1735 (*semblance* for *semblant*) B. seems to reveal a tendency towards modernisation. As indicated in the lists of readings given in Section i., T. frequently differs from F. and is in agreement with G. In this we may see some ground for thinking that the T. text is older than the F. text; but it should be remembered, on the other hand, that T. presents several corruptions that are peculiar to itself (see, *inter alia*, 1858, 1859).

As authorities for the text, they are superior to all the MSS. excepting G. Their value is greatly enhanced by the fact that they are careful transcriptions; for this fact is demonstrable by a close collation of the three texts, which shows conclusively that a very large proportion of their imperfections is to be attributed to their originals.

That these three MSS. are closely related is clear from the following considerations:—

(1) they all omit lines 249, 487, 846, 960, 961, 1490, 1643, 1998, 2338;

(2) they all present the same spurious line in place of 2338;

(3) they all, in place of 2150-53, have a single line made up of the first half of 2150 and the latter half of 2153;

(4) they show the same readings (except in the cases indicated) as the readings of F. given in the lists on pp. 13–15, 19–21;

(5) they exhibit identical, or very similar, defects or corruptions in numerous lines: see, *inter alia*, ll. 793, 994, 1079, 1085, 1269, 1472, 1525, 1798, 1835, 1949, 2092, 2444, 2666-7.

As there is no evidence in support of the hypothesis that any one was copied from any other of these MSS., and as such evidence as exists is against this view, inasmuch as F.B. are sometimes correct when T. is defective* and *vice versâ*, and inasmuch as B. is sometimes sound when F. is unsound and *vice versâ*,* we must conclude, in view of the many agreements between them in the matter of corruptions, omissions, and special readings, that they are descended from a common ancestor.

It is true that there are some divergencies among these MSS., but an inspection of these shows that most of them can with little doubt be ascribed to the natural tendency towards text-corruption that seems to be incidental to the act of transcription; or, in other words, they represent a falling away on the part of one or another MS. from a single model. As the divergencies do not appear to be numerous, and are of a slight character, it may be inferred that the common ancestor of these MSS. was no distant ancestor, and that, consequently, the MSS. are related by near degrees of affinity.

A collation of the MSS. shows that, though F. and T. sometimes agree as against B., or sometimes B. and T. as against F., the most striking differences, and perhaps the most numerous, are when F. and B. agree as against T. In support of this statement I shall offer some evidence. (1) No line in the text, other than those missed by all three, is missed by T. in common with either F. or B., while F. and B. both miss lines 2193, 2475. (2) The variations in the following lines are noticeable:—

638	T. heterly	F.B. hertely
794	T. and	F.B. had
843	T. mote he rente	F.B. mote rente
1099	T. was in his lyue	F.B. was his lyue
1382	T. seite (for *secte*)	F.B. sleighte
1642	T. saued here	F.B. saued there
1736	T. ful of heuynesse	F.B. ful of hevytee
1839	T. were impossible	F.B. hyt were impossible
1987	T. the best rede I can	F.B. the beste rede that I kan
2328	T. loude steuen	F.B. longe stevene
2561	T. and trusteth now in loue	F.B. and as in love truste

In further illustration of the various statements made above, I append an analysis of lines 1548–1615 and 1680–1779, which has been prepared on the lines of the analysis of the readings of G.F.R.A. referred to in the opening of this dissertation. This analysis illustrates the resemblances in orthography and in grammar, the uncertainty of

---

* For illustrations of this statement, see the lists of omitted and transposed lines at the beginning of this article, and also the lists on pp. 51–53.

the scribes as to the value of *e* final, the agreements and divergencies subsisting between F.T.B. It also shows the character of these divergencies, in which we find, most frequently, F. and B. ranged against T. It also illustrates the truth of what has been said above, that there is not much to choose between these three MSS. as authorities for the text, F. presenting 38 and T. and B. each 36 defective lines out of the 168 lines analysed.*

1548	F.—B.—T. F. *Thise Iason*; B. *As Iason (any* for *a)*; T. *And Iason.* T.=G.	1572	F.B.T. All *yrefte*
		1573	F.B.—*T.* T. om. *to hir*, and resembles G. in this defect
1549	F.B.T.		
1550	*F.B.*—T. F.B. om. *he*; F. *yafe*; B.T. *yaf*	1574	F.B.T.
		1575	*F.B.*T. F.B. *al, all* for *alle*
1551	F.B.T.	1576	F.B.T. F.B. *trew*; T. *trewe*
1552	*F.B.*—*T.* F.B. *god wolde*; T. *wolde god.* All insert *that* before *I*	1577	F.B.T. B. *kepte*; F.T. *kept*
		1578	*F.*—B.*T.* F. *and neuer*; B.T. *ne neuer* (=G.) F.T. *joy* for *joye*
1553	F.B.T.		
1554	F.B.T.	1579	F.T.—*B.* B. *and* for *of*
1555	F.B.T. F. *dothe*; B.T. *doth*	1580	F.B.T. F. *Coltes* for *Colcos*
1556	F.B.T.	1581	F.B.T.
1557	F.B.T.	1582	*F.*—*B.T.* F. *nature* for *matier.* All *appeteth* (ith) for *appetiteth*
1558	F.B.T. F.B. *The original*; T. *Thoriginal* (=G)		
1559	F.B.T. F. *sothe*; B.T. *soth.*	1583	*F.*—B.*T.* F. *a hit* for *it*
1560	F.B.T. All *toke*	1584	*F.B.T.* B.T. *welle, wel* for *welle*
1561	F.B.T. F.B. *lyste, luste*; T. *lest*		
		1585	*F.B.*—T. F.B. om. *fals*
1562	F.B.T. F.B. *begate, bigate*	1586	F.B.T.
1563	F.B.T.	1587	F.B.T.
1564	*F.B.T.* All: *sent* for *sente*, and om. *to*	1588	F.B.T.
		1589	F.B.T. F. *forthe*; B.T. *forth*
1565	F.B.T.	1590	*F.B.T.* all *Iasonicos*
1566	F.B.T.	1591	F.—B.—*T.* F.T. *maister*; B. *noble.* T. om. *toun*
1567	F.B.T.		
1568	F.B.—T. F.B. *of*; T. *on.* G. =F.B.	1592	F.B.T. All *y-tolde*
		1593	*F.*—*B.T.* F. *Unto tho otes*; T.B. *Un to otes*
1569	*F.B.*—T. F.B. om. *they*; F. *alle*; B.T. alle		
		1594	F.B.T. F. *most*; T.B. *moste*
1570	*F.B.T.* B.T. couthe for *couthe*	1595	F.B.T. B. *maye*
1571	F.B.T.	1596	F.B.T.

* As F.B. are obviously descended from some MS. now lost, which was not the ancestor of T., and as corruption seems to have been an almost necessary incident in the work of transcription, it might be expected that T. would, in many cases, show readings that are free from corruptions common to F.B. This happens to be the case, and this fact gives T. a special value in the collation of F.T.B. On the other hand, as shown above, T. exhibits many defective and unsound readings of its own. I cannot accept the view of S. Kunz, that of all the MSS. it is nearest to the original.

52 Chaucer's Legend of Good Women

1597	F.B.T. F. *dothe*; B.T. *doth*		1607	F.B.T. corrupt?
1598	F.B.T.		1608	F.B.T.
1599	*F.B.T.* All ins. *so* before *feyre*		1609	F.B.T. All *foule* for *foul*
1600	F.B.T.		1610	F.B.T. F.B. *enamoured* (yd); T. *anamered*
1601	F.B.T.			
1602	*F*.B.T. F. *atte* for *at*		1611	F.B.T. F.T. *quod*; B. *quoth*
1603	F.B.T.		1612	F.B.T.
1604	F.B.T. All *grete*		1613	*F.B.—T.* F.B.T. *and* for *haue*; F.B. *moche, muche*; T. *hugie* (cf. A.γ)
1605	F.T.—B. F.T. *as lyon (lioun)*; B. *as a lioun* (=G)			
1606	F.B.T. F.B. *famulere*; T. *fameler*		1614	F.B.T.
			1615	F.B.T.
1680	F.B.T.		1712	F.B.T.
1681	*F.B.*—T. F.B. *dedes* for *doynges*		1713	F.B.*T*. T. *Colatyns* for *Colatynes*
1682	*F.T.*—B. F.T. *last* for *laste*		1714	F.B.T.
1683	F.B.—T. F.B. *saythe*; T. *seide* (G.=F.B.)		1715	F.B.T. F.T. *knewe*; B. *knew*
			1716	*F.B.T.* All *full prevely*
1684	F.B.T.		1717	F.B.T.
1685	*F.B.*—T. F.B. *to drawen*; T. *and drawen*		1718	F.B.T.
			1719	F.B.T.
1686	*F.B.T.*		1720	F.B.T. T. *ne* for *no*
1687	F.B.T.		1721	*F.B.T.* hypermetrical; T. *soft, wol*
1688	F.B.T. T. *this* for *these*			
1689	*F.T.*—*B.* F.T. om. *he*; B. om. *he that*		1722	F.*B*.T. B. *kepe* for *kepen*
			1723	F.T.—B. B. *to don* for *don*
1690	F.B.T.		1724	F.B.T.
1691	F.B.T. F.B. *starfe*; T. *starue*		1725	F.B.—T. F.B. *sayne, seyn*; T. *seith* (T.=G.)
1692	F.B.—*T*. T. om. *wise*			
1693	B.*T*. T. *touch* for *touche*; F. omits line		1726	F.B.T. F. *werne fal*; B. *weryn fall*; T. *weryn fallen*
1694	F.B.T.			
1695	F.B.T.		1727	F.B.T.
1696	F.B.T. All *wroughten* (v. sp.)		1728	F.B.T.
1697	F.B.T. All *thoughten* (v. sp.)		1729	F.B.—*T*. T. *with-in, stinteth* for *with, stingeth*?
1698	F.B.T.			
1699	F.B.—*T*. T. om. *of*		1730	*F.B.T.* All *these* for *the sege*
1700	*F.B.T.* B.T. *seide*		1731	*F.*—B.T. F. *my* for *his*
1701	*F.B.T.* All om. *no*; T. *this* for *his*		1732	F.B.T. All *wepe*
			1733	F.B.T. All *toke*
1702	F.B.T.		1734	*F*.B.T. F. *mekly* for *mckely*
1703	*F.B.T*. F. *hem* for *him*; T. *prey* for *preyse*		1735	F.B.T. F.T. *semblant*; B. *semblance*
1704	F.*B.T*. B. *spech*; T. *speche*		1736	*F.B.*—*T*. F.B. *hevytee*; T. *heuynesse* for *honeste*; F. *the* for *her*
1705	*F.B.T.* F.B. *hyght*; T. *hat* for *hyghte*			
1706	*F.B.*—T. F.B. *for*; T. *sir*; B. *seid* (T.=G.)		1737	F.B.T. T. *embelesed*
			1738	F.B.T. F. *hert* for *herte*
1707	F.B.T.		1739	*F.B.*—*T*. F.B. *acordeden* hypermetrical; T. *acordyn*
1708	F.T.—B. F.T. *quod*; B. *quoth*			
1709	F.B.*T*. T. *hirde* for *hire*			
1710	F.B.T.		1740	F.B.T.
1711	F.B.T.		1741	F.B.T. T. *stertyn* for *stertyng*

1742	F.B.T.	1763	*F.*—B.T. F. *this, thys*; B.T. *thus, thus*
1743	F.B.T. B. *uprose*		
1744	F.B.T. All *kyssed*	1764	F.B.T. F.T. *hert*
1745	F.B.*T.* T. *kyng* for *kynges*	1765	F.B.T.
1746	F.B.T.	1766	F.B.T.
1747	*F.B.T.* All *bounte* for *shap*	1767	F.B.T.
1748	F.B.T.	1768	F.B.T.
1749	F.B.T.	1769	F.B.T.
1750	*F.B.T.* All *kaught* for *kaughte*	1770	F.B.T.
1751	*F.B.T.* F.T. *hert, brent*	1771	F.B.T.
1752	*F.B.T.* All om. *al*	1772	F.B.T. B. *me* for *my*
1753	*F.B.*T. B. *shuld* for *shulde*	1773	F.B.T. B. *quoth*; F.T. *quod*
1754	F.B.T. All om. *that*	1774	F.B.T.
1755	F.—B.T. F. *he covetyth*; T.B. om. *he*	1775	F.B.T. F.T. *gyrt, girt*
		1776	*F.T.*—*B.* F.T. *he forth right* for *forth he rit*; B. is corrupt and inverts ll. 1776, 1777
1756	F.B.T.		
1757	F.B.T.		
1758	F.B.T.		
1759	F.B.T.	1777	F.B.—*T.* T. *that he hath* for *then hath he*
1760	F.B.T.		
1761	F.B.T.	1778	F.B.T.
1762	F.T.—B. F.T. *this was*; B. *thus was* (B.=G.)	1779	F.B.T.

The examination of the texts of these MSS. points to the conclusion that F. and B. are copies—possibly first-hand copies—of some older MS., the text of which was itself descended from the still earlier text which was the common ancestor of all three MSS. It is not possible to state how many copies intervened between this common ancestor and F. and B. on the one hand, and T. on the other, but we may feel confident that there was at least one between it and F.B. By a collation of B. and F., we might obtain inductively a fairly accurate reproduction of the text of their immediate predecessor, and by a collation of F.B. and T. we could arrive inductively at a knowledge of the state of the text of their common ancestor. In both cases, it is evident the texts would present numerous imperfections, though, of course, there would be more in the former than in the latter of these.

All three MSS. agree in giving the spurious line (see 2339 in F.T.B.)—

    Huge (F. huges) ben thy sorwes and wonder smerte (F. smert).

and also the following readings :—

1386 For they shal haue wel better and gretter chere.
1472 Where lay the ship (F. shippe) that Iason gan arryve.
1835 A worde for shame ne may she forthe out brynge.
1949 Unto the contree of kyng (F.B. kynge) Mynos full of myght.

In these instances, the text appears to have been corrupted by an editor unrestrained by diffidence, and caution is therefore necessary in dealing with the peculiar readings of F.T.B. It is by no means improbable that several of the readings (see pp. 13-15, 19-21) characteristic of the F.T.B. group should be included in the category of unauthorised modifications of the text.

This discussion suggests three important considerations which should be kept in view in the preparation of a critical text of the L.G.W. In the first place, though these three MSS. possess a high authority, they cannot be accepted as transcripts of a text which had received the approval of the poet, and were representative of his final intentions. In the second place, before a reading of any one of these MSS. be accepted, it should be compared with the readings of its two fellows. In the third place, a reading which is common to all three of these MSS., while it undoubtedly derives considerable authority from the fact that it must be the reading of some older and less corrupted MS., should not be regarded as the reading of three independent MSS., but as the reading of *one* MS., whose merits must be weighed against the readings of other independent MSS., if such exist.

MS. Arch. Selden. B. 24, Bodleian Library.—This MS. presents the revised form of the Prologue, and an almost complete text of the legends. It has lost a leaf, involving the loss of lines 2551-2616, and, moreover, omits lines 860, 861, 960, 961, 1568-71, 2226, 2227.

The orthography of the MS. betrays Scottish proclivities in the scribe. He writes *quh* for *wh* in such words as *wh*ich, *wh*en, *wh*at, *wh*ether, etc.; *nocht* for *nat*, *ane* for *oon*, *outher* for *eyther*, *airly* for *erly* (early). Further, he seems to prefer the spelling *ith* to *eth* in the inflexions of the verb, and almost invariably changes *her* and *hem* into *thaire* and *thame*.

Language and rhythm show that the importance of the *e* final in Chaucer's metrical system was not understood by the Scotchman who, in l. 118, writes: *Upon the small soft suete gras,* and whose text offers many examples of the insertion or substitution of words in lines which were evidently considered defective in the number of their syllables. For example, *trewe* not being recognised as a dissyllable, line 560:—*Ne shal no trewe louer come in helle*—is emended by the substitution of *never* for *no*.

The text of this MS. has been so largely edited (see a bold but unhappy change in ll. 2010, 2011) that the readings, when unsupported, must always be viewed with suspicion. On the other hand, the scribe evidently endeavoured to understand the author he was transcribing, as he rarely misses the sense. The text seems to be superior to that of R., and is of considerable value for purposes of collation.

As regards the relations of this MS., it has been shown that it is distinguished from G. by presenting what have been described as the revised readings. On the other hand, it is alone among the MSS. in confirming the readings of G. in lines 238, 317, 404, 805, 1129, 1221, 1296, 1387, 1523, 1596, but, as in these G.A. have perhaps preserved the correct readings, their resemblances cannot be accepted as evidence of special kinship.

When collated with F.T.B. in respect to their omissions, and the readings given on pp. 13–15, 19–21, it is clearly distinguished from this group. On the other hand, in a few instances A. presents readings which are found in the members of the F.T.B. group, and some of which are also found in P.γ, *e.g.*:—

258   *boughten* F.T.B.P. (this plural is perhaps wrong, as the statement seems to apply to Polixene, and not to Lucrece).
1107 *pauementis* F.T.B.P.Rl. (G. *ornementis*).
1547 *entent* F.T.B.γ. (G.R. *assent*; as Prof. Skeat points out, *intent* does not give a correct rime).
1613 *Ye haue your self y-put in huge dout* T.γ. (T. *and* for *haue* in error)
1659 *a cheif traytour* F.T.B. (G. *thef and traytour*; R. *a. a thyef traytour*).
2277 *Myself with hir I wole* F.T.B. β.γ. (G.R. *Myn self with hyre wele*).

These specific resemblances, to mention only the more striking ones, are few and scattered. As they cannot well be regarded as the result of accident and, in some cases, without doubt involve corruptions, they are, perhaps, to be accounted for on the hypothesis that, in A., readings have been incorporated which were borrowed from some MS. of the type of F.T.B., or of the type of γ., or of some other type unknown to us.

While A. is to be distinguished from G. on the one side, and the members of the F.T.B. group on the other, it seems to possess certain special relationships with β. and R. Its kinship to β. will not be

56 Chaucer's Legend of Good Women

here illustrated, as the subject is discussed in the article on β. Its relations with R. require some investigation.

It has been shown* that R. and A. may be regarded as presenting generally the same type of text, and that they are frequently in agreement in readings which are different from the corresponding readings presented by G. and F. in common or separately. A few selected illustrations of these agreements between R. and A. are here offered.

346 R.A. But of his *det* he *shuld* be stable (F. *deitee, shal*).
616 R.A. The weddyng and the fest(e) *for* to dyuyse (*editing*. G.F. om. *for*).
666 R.A. Ye men that *sweren falsly* many an othe (G.F. *falsely swere*).
775 R.A. Had dryed up the dew of *herbys swete* (F.G. *herbes wete*).
868 R.A. That hyt was Piramus hyr hert *so* dere (*editing*. G. *herte dere*).
910 R.A. But God forbede but *yef* a woman can (*editing*. G.F. om. *yef*).
1062 R.A. And had herd *ofter* (A. *oftar*) of Eneas *then* tho (*editing*. G.F. *ofte*; *er*).
1215 R.A. That I myght ones mete hym with thys spere (G.F. *hym onys mete*. Probably R.A. here correct).
1370 R.A. Of *gentyl* wemen *tendre* creatures (G. *tendere, gentil*; F. *gentil, gentil*).
1382 R.A. *set, sett* for *secte*.
1400 R.A. Eson (G.F. *Pelleus*), but differ in the line.
1457 R.A. Let hym *go* rede Argomauticon (A. Argonaucion; *editing*. G.F. om. *go*).
1495 R.A. And com *to* (A. for to) *play vs out* of the see (G.F. *for to pleye out*).
1597 R.A. And *dyd* hym honour as hyt *was* to don (*editing*. G.F. *doth*: G. *was*; F. *is*).
1674 R.A. Why lyked me thy *thought* (G.F. *youthe*. A. is here unlike β.).
1876 R.A. And *for* the stable hert (F. *in*).
2676 R.A. *Danao* for *Lino* (but the readings are different.)

Examples might be multiplied, but the above are sufficient for the purpose. It will be observed that, in several of the examples above given, the text has been edited for the purpose of obtaining a verse of five measures in cases where Chaucer's verse system was not understood; and it will also be observed that, in some instances, the changes are such as might have suggested themselves independently to different minds. The mere fact, therefore, that we should find two MSS. in occasional agreement in such cases cannot fairly be adduced as evidence of their kinship. On the other hand,

* See p. 33.

when we find a large number of such coincidences, and observe that these are accompanied by coincidences in blunders, it is impossible to resist the conviction that the texts in these MSS., if not related by common descent, at least stand to one another in the relation of debtor and creditor.

If we adopt the hypothesis of common descent, it will be necessary to define this hypothesis more precisely and surround it with certain qualifications. In the first place, the common ancestor from which R. and A. may have inherited their common corruptions cannot be placed very far back in time, for, from the nature of these corruptions, it must have been a late copy of the text—later, probably, than the members of the F.T.B. group. Again, as the differences between R. and A. in the matter of edited and corrupted readings are perhaps more numerous than the resemblances, we must assume, if these divergent corruptions took place at later stages of transcription, that there were at least one or two such stages between the common ancestor and R. on the one side and A. on the other. Further, it has been pointed out that the resemblances between R. and A. almost disappear in the later legends, while the divergencies in the matter of corruption are more numerous and more striking. A few resemblances between R. and A. may still be noticed, but some of these may be purely accidental, while in others—as in 2379 ($\beta.\gamma.$), 2445, 2484 ($\beta.\gamma.$), 2632—R. A. give what is possibly the right reading, and their agreement cannot be adduced as evidence of relationship. But even these resemblances are as nothing in comparison with such divergencies as we find in lines 2314, 2317, 2327, 2328, 2370, 2388, 2389, 2393, 2409, 2433, 2487, 2489, 2621, 2637, 2649, 2679, to mention a few of them. In view of these facts, the hypothesis should not be held to apply to the later legends.

There is, on the other side, something to be said in favour of the alternative hypothesis that these resemblances between R. and A., or a good number of them, may be regarded as the result of borrowings at the different stages of transcription which terminated in the text in A. It is by no means improbable that, by the middle of the fifteenth century, there were several copies in existence of the L.G.W. and other poems of Chaucer, and it is reasonable to suppose that two or three copies were accessible to individuals wishing to make a new transcription. If these copies presented different types of text, it is easy to understand how variations might be introduced which would tend to the differentiation of types. Such differentiation can be seen to have taken place in the case of Thynne's printed edition, a century later, and possibly the same process was at work in the evolution of the γ. text. Now, it has already been shown that A. may have borrowed from other MSS. some of the readings which differentiate it from G. and R., and if there was borrowing from one quarter, there may have been borrowing from another.

A. occasionally offers a reading which, if not the correct one, is sometimes the best and generally merits consideration.

903	That in a graue we mote bothe lye (confirmed by Ff.; see R.a.).
1046	That neuer yet was sene so fremd a cas (unique).
1203	That helith seke folk of nyghtis sorowe (B).
1353	Quhan she was hurt before that she deid (a.).
1360	Syn that the goddes ben contrair to me (unique). G.R. *contrarye*).
1449	And chese quhat folk that thou wilt with the take (unique).
1489	For of socour they schulde nothing faile.
1538	As wolde almychti god that I had geue (unique).
1613	Ye haue your self yput in huge dout (cf. T.γ.).
1649	And gatt him name rycht as a conquerour (β.).
2068	That I mote of a traytour haue a name (unique).
2094	It is no proffer as to your kinrede (unique).
2102	Ye suere it here on all that may be suorn (β.γ.).
2215	For though so be that any bote her come (β.).

Also see lines 1259, 1263, 1345, 1366, 1927, 1964, 1999, 2655, referred to on pp. 25, 26.

MS. R. 3.19, *in the Library of Trin. Coll., Camb., on paper.*—This MS. contains the revised draft of the Prologue and all the legends, including the Hypermnestra fragment, but omits the following lines: 233, 234, 332, 333, 489, 960, 961, 1627, 2202, 2203, 2287-92, 2569. Moreover, it inverts the order of ll. 251, 252; 1732, 1733; 2016, 2017.

This must be a late transcript. The language on almost every page shows that the importance of *e* final in Chaucer's grammatical and metrical system was not understood, words being frequently introduced in order to make up the necessary number of syllables in lines which, owing to the non-vocalisation of *e*, were evidently considered defective. Further, the diction and grammar exhibit *modernisation*. Almost invariably *aldermost* is replaced by *princi-*

Chaucer's Legend of Good Women

pally, *natheles* by *neuerthelesse*, *quod* by *quoth*, while *am*, *is*, *was* frequently take the place of *nam*, *nis*, *nas* respectively, and *that* takes the place of *thilke*. The verbal prefix *y* is often dropped (see 6, 26, 204, 219, 222, etc.); verbal inflexions frequently disappear, e.g. *forther* for *forthren*, *usyd* for *useden*, *do* for *doon*, *mot* for *moten*. Again, strong verbs sometimes become weak, e.g. *dyd wepe* for *wep* (1732), *agrysyd* for *agros* (2314). Moreover, there is considerable uncertainty in the employment of the forms of the pronoun of the third person, e.g.—Had found *her* lord *theyr* governour * (1060). In these examples dialectic habit seems to have led away the scribe.

The text, as we find it in this MS., has been unsparingly edited. Numerous examples of this are to be met with on every page, but, as some of these are given in the article dealing with A, it is not necessary to offer any here.

In view of what has been said, it is evident that the text in this MS. has a restricted value, but it is useful for purposes of collation. It seems to be somewhat less corrupt than α., a MS. to which, as will be shown, it is nearly akin. Moreover, it frequently confirms the readings of other MSS., and occasionally offers a reading which, if not the true reading, is sometimes the best, and merits consideration.

 336 ffor though that thow renyed hast my lay (unique).
 493 That he hys seruantes charge by eny way (α.).
 903 That in oon graue i-fere we moten ly (also in α., but see A.).
1046 That neuer was ther yet so frende (for *fremde*) a cas (Th.).
1055 And when they haddyn told all theyr (for *her*) dystres (γ.).
1091 And commandyd theyr messyngers to go (T.Th.).
1099 He neuer better at ease was in hys lyue (confirms T. P.γ.).
1174 And eke so lykly for to be a man (α.P.Rl.).
1203 That heleth folkes of hyr nyghtys sorow (α.).
1210 And forth this nobyll quene thus lat I ryde (α.).
1499 And fynt thys lason and thys other stonde (unique).
1716 And pryuyly in to the hous they gone (see α.).
1755 The more he couetyd hyr and thought hyr fayre (see β.γ.).
1824 Allas of the thys was a veleyns dede (α.γ.).
1847 And they answeredyn all opon theyr fay (unique).
1881 Nat so gret feyth in all that he ne fonde (see α. which om. *ne*).
1897 To Atenes of whych hyt happyd thus (γ.).
1936 Vnto Minos to saue hym or to spyll (α.).

* Examples are numerous.

1967 But I not how hit happyd there percace (*a.*).
2007 And then anon when that Theseus sethe (unique).
2215 ffor though so be that shyp or boot hyr come (A.β. better).
2396 That may ye fynde yef that hyt lyke yow (confirms B.γ.).
2712 And from hys wyfe he ran a full good pas (β.).

It has been shown—(1) that R. presents a revised text of the legends; (2) that it is as distinct from G. as it is from the F. type of MS.; (3) that R. may be said to occupy a kind of middle position between them; (4) that when it agrees with neither F. nor G., but offers an unique reading, or one supported only by A., its readings, with few exceptions, are open to suspicion.

The relations of R. and A. have been discussed in the article on the latter MS. Its relations with *a.* will be illustrated in the article on *a.*

Additional MS. 9832, *British Museum on paper, said to be of the middle of the* 15*th century.*—This MS. contains the revised form of the Prologue, and also the legends of Cleopatra, Thisbe, Dido, Medea, Lucrece, and a portion of the legend of 'Adryane' down to l. 1985 on the last leaf of the MS.

This MS. omits ll. 166, 233, 234, 332, 333, 351, 629, 630 (it has here a line made up of portions of 629, 630), 865-872, 960, 961, 1255, 1517, 1744-6, 1783, 1895, 1945. Moreover, it inverts the order of ll. 766, 767; 1566, 1567; 1732, 1733.

It will presently be shown that this MS. closely resembles R., the Trinity Coll. MS., of which, allowance being made for corruptions peculiar to each, it may be regarded as a duplicate. Much of what was said in respect to the modernisation of the language of the R. text (see above) is applicable to this MS. as well. The British Museum MS. has been ascribed to the middle, and the Trinity College MS. to the end, of the 15th century. From a comparison of the two, I am inclined to think that the former exhibits a greater number of defective lines and corruptions than the latter, but this consideration, while it may justify some scepticism as to the soundness of the views expressed as to the respective periods at which each MS. was written, does not, on the other hand, afford sufficient ground for rejecting these views. R. perhaps reveals a more strongly-marked tendency to substitute more modern for archaic expressions, and *a.* gives correctly *deyte* in 346, and *secte* in 1382, but the differences in the language of the texts presented by them do not appear to be sufficiently marked to enable us to arrive at any satisfactory conclusion on the subject.

I offer the following reasons for the purpose of showing the connexion between these two MSS. Both R. and *a*.—

(1.) agree in the omission of the lines 233, 234, 332, 333, 960, 961;

(2.) invert the order of lines 1732, 1733;

(3.) agree in numerous readings, involving guesses and corruptions, which could hardly have suggested themselves independently to different minds. A few examples are: 95 R. *hertly*, *a*. *hertely* (for *erthely*); 109 R.*a*. *gret* (for *glad*), 265 R. *Candace*, *a*. *Caudas* (for Canace); 515 R.*a*. *restoryd* (for *rescued*); 1373, R.*a*. *versyd* (for *farsed*); 1381 R.*a*. *youe* (for *shoue*);

232 Therwith methought I saw a selcouth syght.
480 ffor thy trespas to put the out of were.
545 And hyt was preuyd in dede doyng.
716 Of all that lond he was oon of the best.
735 ffor loue ys feruent and hatter than the fyre (G. as wry the glede and hettere is the fyr).
1052 ⎱ Vnto the tempyll there for to beseke (*a*. *in-to* and om. *for*)
1053 ⎰ The quene and (*a*. of) hyr socour that ys so meke.
1662–1665 That ys *hys* mede of loue and guerdone (G.T. *the*)
That *fayre* Medea receueth (*a*. receyvid) of Iasone (G.F. om. *fayre*)
Ryght for hyr trouthe and hyr *gentylnes* (G.F. *kyndenesse*)
That louyd hym bettyr than *hymself* I ges (G.F. *hire self*).

Now, as R. frequently gives a correct reading when *a*. is defective, and *a*. a correct reading when R. is defective, it is not open to us to hold that one is a copy of the other, and, in view of the common omissions, transposition, and corruptions, we must conclude that both R. and *a*. are closely related, and almost duplicate copies of some lost MS. It is evident that this lost MS. must itself have been full of modernisations, omissions, and other corruptions. To these inherited corruptions each MS. adds a considerable number of its own. It should be added that, though the differences that exist between these MS. are numerous, this fact is in no way inconsistent with the theory of common descent, for each copyist may have run his individual course of blundering and editing. For example, there can be little difficulty in guessing the origin of such variations as :—

52 R. Of hit to do all reuerence (F. doon it all).
a. Off hit to don hit all maner reuerence (see A.).

85	R. That in thys derk world me wynt and ledeth.
	a. That in this derke world me gydith or ledyth (see A.).
1706, 1707	R. And sayd thus nay *syr* hyt ys no nede
	To *trow* on the worde but on the dede.
	a. And said thus naye *for* hit is no nede
	To *trowyn* on the worde but on the dede.
1870	R. Syth *that* day and she was *holdyn* there.
	a. Seth *thyke* (thilke) daye and she was *hold* there.

If we refer to the lists of readings on pp. 29, 30, showing special agreements between R. and A., we find that with few exceptions a., so far as it extends, presents the same readings as these MSS. In 346 a. reads *deyte, shuld*; 868 a. is wanting; 910 a. shows *yf* but omits *but*; 1382 a. gives *secte* correctly for R.A. *set*; 1400 a. reads *Esoon*, but agrees with R. and not with A.

Curiously enough, a. agrees with A., and not with R., in lines:

52	a.A. *all maner reuerence.*
85	a. *gydith or ledyth*; A. *gyeth and ledeth*; R. *me wynt and ledeth.*
186	a.A. *befall*; R. *fall.*
454	a.A. *God*; R. *go.*
1009	a.A. *quenes the floure*; R. *quenes floure.*
1353	a.A. *before that*; R. *beforn er.*
1401	a.A. *realme*; R. *reygne.*
1437	a.A. *and with the dragon*; R. *and the dragon.*

These resemblances suggest the view that A. may be more closely connected with a. than with R, but the evidence affords an insufficient basis for anything more than mere hypothesis. It is enough for our purposes to recognise the existence of the broad fact that a. is closely related to R., and that some special relationship subsists between A. and the group R.a.

This MS. confirms the R. readings in ll. 493, 903, 1174, 1203, 1210, 1716, 1824, 1881 (imperfect), 1936, 1967: see these readings in the article on R. In 1353, a. agrees with A. in providing what is at least an intelligible reading. In 1382, a. alone confirms G. in the word *secte*, which is undoubtedly the right reading. a. offers, in 1386, an excellent reading—*ffor they shall haue bettyr loue and chere*; in 1839, what is probably the correct reading—*The wo to tellyn wer an inpossible*; see p. 113.

Additional MS. 28617, in the British Museum.—Several leaves of this MS. have been lost, and some injured. It presents a small

Chaucer's Legend of Good Women 63

portion of the Prologue, portions of the legends of Cleopatra, Thisbe, Dido, Lucrece, Ariadne, and complete, or nearly complete, transcripts of the legends of Medea (ll. 1516, 1517 missing), "Philomene," Phyllis, and Hypermnestra.

It is a comparatively modern transcript. Final *e* generally occurs in the right place, and is almost always correctly shown in the rimewords. On the other hand, it is sometimes omitted in such verbs as *wyst* (853), *must* (933), *myght* (935), *lyst* (996), though required by the metre, and, moreover, is often inserted when not required by grammar or metre, as in *bloode* (874), *warme, hoote* (914), *gladde* (961). Further, not infrequently the scribe shows that he is unable to appreciate the rhythm of Chaucer's verse (see lines 1009, 1696, 1697, 1906, etc.).

It is also important to observe that the scribe occasionally lapses into what seems to be dialectic habit, for he substitutes *es* for *eth* in the inflexion of the 3rd person singular, present tense (see 1729, 1942); in 847 he writes *na mare* for *no more*, and in 1872 *theyre* for *her*.

Except in the case of lines 960, 961, which it includes, this MS. presents none of the readings in G. which, it has been suggested, underwent revision. As the surviving fragments of the MS. present most of the revised lines, it must be classed with the texts showing revision.

If we compare the readings of γ. with the readings of G.F.R.A. given on pp. 4-7, 9-12, we find that γ.—

(1) generally agrees with, or supports, the readings of F.R.A. in the G.—F.R.A. list;

(2) agrees with, or supports, most of the F.A. or the F.R. readings in the G.—F.R.—F.A.—R.A. list.

N.B.—For F.A., see lines 587, 831, 938, 963, 1160, 1475, 1977, 2370, 2430, 2469, 2639, 2706.
For F.R., see lines 870, 1324, 1352, 1449, 1570, 1973, 2358, 2563, 2579, 2601.
For R.A., see line 1993.

It will be seen that γ. seldom agrees with G. when the readings of this MS. are unsupported by other MSS. Agreements with G. are to be noticed in lines 853, 1074, 1427, 1593, 1597, 1626, 1779 (also β.), 1951 (see A.), 1995, 2291, 2350 (also β.), 2378, 2395 (also β.), 2476, 2534, 2546, 2717; but, in these instances, G. seems to offer the correct reading, and they cannot, therefore, be adduced as evidence that any special kinship subsists between the text in G. and that in γ. It is true that γ. presents lines 960, 961, which are found only in G.P.Rl. besides, but no weight can be attached to this circumstance in the presence of the overwhelming evidence above adduced, which makes it impossible for us to admit any relationship between G. and γ.

If, now, we compare the readings of γ. with the readings of G.F.R.A. given on pp. 13-15, 19-21, we find that γ.—

(1) generally agrees with, or supports, the readings of G.R.A. in the F.—G.R.A. list;

(2) agrees with, or supports, most of the G.A. or G.R. or R.A. readings in the F.—G.R.—G.A.—R.A. list.

N.B.—For G.R., see lines 1559, 1801, 1940, 2032, 2226, 2286, 2503, 2511, 2583, 2603, 2648.

For G.A., see lines 1002, 1053, 1764, 2046, 2239, 2291, 2452, 2477.

For R.A., see lines 1217 (*the* for *these*), 1251, 1857, 1886, 2507.

It is evident, therefore, that the text in γ. is to a great extent distinct from the text in F. On the other hand, it presents several examples of resemblance to the F.T.B. type of text, some of which are particularly striking: see lines 1345, 1357, 1362, 1370, 1472, 1652, 1653, 1668, 1671, 1773, 1969, 1971, 2030, 2084, 2255, 2525, 2592, 2652. In addition, F.T.B. and γ. exhibit similar corruptions in lines 903, 1524, 1564, 2111, and for lines 2338, 2339, read:—

O sely Phylomene woo ys thyn herte
Huge ben thy sorwes and wondre smerte (as in γ).

Moreover, further investigation shows that γ. is more in accordance with T. than with the other members of the F.T.B. group: see lines 1382, γ. *seeyte*, T. *seite*; 1548, γ.T. *and*, F. *thise*, B. *as*; 1568, *on his children*; 1613, *huge*; 1649, *hym a name*; 1962, *to, to*; 2001, *haue* for *saue*; 2328, *lowde stevene*.

In view of the circumstances above stated, it would appear that γ. occupies a position intermediate between G. and F.; that, for the greater part, it presents a type of text showing affinities to the type of text from which it may be supposed R. or A. was derived; but that it is much nearer to the F.T.B. type than R. or even A., which, it has been shown, presents a few resemblances to the

F.T.B. group. However, it must be observed that, except in the case of the lines resembling the F.T.B. type, many of which would appear to involve corruptions, γ. is on the whole decidedly superior to R. or A. or their congeners, as it presents far fewer corruptions or examples of editing. If the list of corruptions and editings of R. and A. given on pp. 29, 30 be inspected, it will be found that γ. shows similar corruptions only in lines 910, 1062, 1457, 1520. It also shows readings similar to those met with in R. or A. or a. in lines 1009, 1030, 1065, 1094, 1407, 1476, 1760, 1777, 1981, 2072, 2179, 2426. Some of these resemblances may, however, be accidental, and it is worthy of notice that, generally, γ. is in agreement with, or supports, the F.G. readings in the A.—G.F.—G.R.—F.R. and the R.—G.F.—G.A.—F.A. readings given on pp. 25, 26: see lines 866, 1010, 1366, 1743, 2068, 2327, 2655.

In view of the fragmentary character of this MS. it is difficult to arrive at any satisfactory conclusion in respect to the history of its text. The fact that the text in γ. seems to jump suddenly from readings of one type to readings of another type suggests the view that this text is of a hybrid or composite character, and that the transcriber of the MS., or the transcriber of some earlier MS. from which it was derived, had before him two or more MSS. of different types. On the other hand, as γ. shows many readings which are superior even to those of the F.T.B. group (*e.g.* see 1736, 1739), it might be inferred that it was copied directly from some transcript of the poem earlier even than the lost ancestor of F.T.B., and, in view of its many resemblances to the readings presented by this group, it is possible that this earlier transcript was in some manner related to the common ancestor of F.T.B.

From what has been said it is obvious that γ. is a very interesting and important MS., and its fragmentary character is to be regretted.

Additional MS., 12,524, *in the British Museum.*—This begins at l. 1640 and continues to the end of the Hypermnestra fragment. An injured leaf preserves only fragments of lines 2455–2461.

In respect to its spelling, *F* is frequently doubled, even when not used as a capital letter, e.g. *wyff, selff,* etc.; also *s*, e.g. *wass, sso. Yh* is used for *y*, as *yhe* (ye), *yher* (yer); *w* for *u* and *v*, as in *wnder* (under), *dewoured*. There is also a quaint-looking word, *thewichely* (1781 = thievishly).

Chaucer's use of the *e* final, though this letter is often written where it is required by grammar and metre, would appear to have been not understood by the scribe. In the language of the MS., a tendency to modernise is noticeable. *Shapede* is used for the p.p. *shapen*, 2692; *ar* takes the place occasionally of *ben*, while *them* and *ther* repeatedly take the place of *hem* and *her*. The scribe almost regularly writes *ane* for *one*, and *awne* for *owen*.

There are many bad and corrupt lines in the MS., and the individual responsible for the text has not resisted the temptation to *edit* or *amend*. Glaring instances of this may be found in ll. 1772, 1773, 2543, 2544, 2696, 2697; in some of which the rhythm is sadly violated.

On the whole, however, the MS., though evidently a late transcript, presents, comparatively speaking, a good copy of the poem, and is useful for purposes of collation. The following readings merit notice :—

1649   And gat hym name right as a conqueroure (confirms A.).
1659   As euer in loue traytour and theffe he was (unique).
1686   The wertuouse wyff the werie lucrese. (unique.)
1701   confirms G., but order of words changed.
1755   The more he coueyteth hyr and thoght hyr feyre. (γ. and see R.)
1830   like G., *usyn* for *used* of all the other texts.
1837   But at the last off torquyne she hem tolde. (unique.)
1839   tends to confirm the reading of R.A. (*were an impossible*).
2019   And when that he this monstre hath ourecome. (unique.)
2092   Then that I suffred giltelese you sterwe. (confirms G.)
2199   Hadde he nat syn that hyr thus begylde. (confirms G.A.γ.)
2592   Then what with wenus and other oppressioune. (confirms G.)

Tested by the G. readings given in Section ii., this MS. must be classed with those presenting a revised text of the poem, for in no one instance does it present any of these readings.

Tested by the F. readings given in the lists on pp. 13–15, 19–21, the text in β. shows that it has no kinship with the F.T.B. group. It does confirm the reading of these MSS. in ll. 1671, 1710, 2030; but these readings seem to be the correct ones.*

If β. is distinct from G. on the one side and F. on the other, there can be no doubt about its near kinship to A., of which it

* It also shows a few resemblances in: 1764, *new* for *now*; 1801, *men a woman*; 2126, *and* for *al*; 2488, *delyuer hyr*; 2648, *espe*; but these might be accidental.

is practically a duplicate, due allowance being made for differences of spelling and dialectic peculiarities. This is established by a comparison of the readings in—

1741 Or she wes off him war come starteling in.
1743 And she anone arose with humble chere.
1841 As hadde ffolkes hertes be made off stones.
2299 And grete me wele the doughter that is thi viffe.

And also see, *inter alia*, ll. 1649, 1776, 1826, 1906, 1940, 1992, 1999, 2083, 2084, 2132, 2163, 2253, 2263, 2328, 2357, 2358, 2503.

In 1739, *worde* for *dede*; 2003, *thereto* for *also*; β. presents what may be accidental resemblances to R. Its relations generally to the other MSS. follow those of A.

Pepys MS., 2006, *in the Magdalen Coll. Lib., Camb. Univ.*—This MS. presents ll. 1-1377. Lines 777 to 845 are in a different handwriting from the rest of the *Legend of Good Women*. In the Prologue, which is in the revised form, ll. 232, 437 are missing; line 251 becomes 249, and a spurious line replaces the former. The *Legend of Cleopatra* lacks l. 623; in the *Legend of Thisbe*, owing to missing leaves in the MS., ll. 706-776 are lost; in the *Legend of Dido*, l. 1275 is missing; there are only 10 lines of the *Legend of Medea*.

This is a poor MS., the text of which obviously belongs to a time when Chaucer's grammatical system was obsolete. The corruptions of the text—towards which probably several successive transcribers had contributed—are many and outrageous. Many of the lines make absolute nonsense, while we find such specimens of Chaucer's verse as the following:—

601 For the love of the lady dame Cleopatrace.
857 Thann may he me hold falls and vnkynde.
1184 But her of was betwyn hem so longe a sermonynge
1185 The wheche were to longe for to mak ther-of rehersynge.
1376 And thow wer not fals to oon but thow wer fals to twoo.

The arbitrary changes that have been made in the text deprive the MS. of any real value for purposes of systematic collation, though, of course, many of the original lines seem to have been preserved, and confirm the readings of one or another of the remaining MSS. It would certainly be unwise to accept any reading of P. that is not supported by more reliable MSS.

Tested by the readings of G. given in Section ii., this MS. shows that it belongs to the group of MSS. giving a revised draft of the poem; for, with the exception of ll. 960, 961, it is found in no instance to agree with G. In other respects, it seems to occupy a position somewhat nearer to G. than even R. and A. In the Prologue it is, of course, more in accordance with F. than with G., but even here it has curious resemblances to G. in minor matters, *e.g.* 313, *hym herd* (G. only); 449, *what* (G.A.α.); 482, *lif* (G. only). In the legends, it reveals agreements with G. in 636, *payned* (G. only); 671, *wolde* (G. only); 694, *be well seen* (G.α., corrupt); 793, *hast(e)* for *lykynge* (G.Ff.); 831, *herte* for *heer* (G.Th.); 871, *tournement* for *tormente* (G.); 874, *med(e)led* (G. only); 882, *he* (G.α.); 960, 961 occur only in G.γ.Rl.P.; 1074, *he semed* (G.α.γ.Rl.); 1119, *shined* (G.T. only); 1135, *presentes*; 1139, *But neth(e)les our autour telleth thus* (G. *us* for *thus*); 1187, *thyng* (G.Rl.); 1235 *chaunge hir* (G.Rl.). It may be said that these readings are the results of accident, but the resemblances are too numerous to justify such a hypothesis.

Again, it presents resemblances to MSS. of the R. and α. type, *e.g.* ll. 777, 800, 801, 932, 980, 1076, 1147, 1217, which are all similarly corrupt. While in ll. 336, omission of *that*; 345, *be this* (thus); 371, *and though*; 403, *it so be*; 404, *dredeful hert*; 435, *and that blive*; 436, *neuer* for *no*; 459, corrupt, but omits *geue me*; 1107, *pavements* for *ornements*; 1269, *To hir at festes and at dauntes*; 1296, *me so sore* for *so sore me*; 1339, *Tak my sowle and vnbynd me of this vnrest* (see T.); 1345, *So grete rewth I have it for to endite*; 1357, *I make* for *make I*; 1370, *of Ientil women and Ientil creatures*,—the Pepys MS. shows relationship to MSS. of the F.T.B. type. In ll. 853, 1019, there are two misreadings which may have come from B., which is the only other MS. in which they occur.

In view of the facts stated, it would appear that P. must be regarded as a hybrid or composite text, to the evolution of which a MS. of the type of G. and another of the F.T.B. type perhaps contributed.

Rawlinson MS., C. 86, Bodleian Library. On paper; of the 16*th century* (*Bod. Lib. MSS. Catal.*). This MS. contains only the *Legend of Dido*, which, apparently, has been ascribed by somebody to "Lidgate," as this name occurs in the margin opposite to the first line.

The MS. misses l. 1067, and inverts the order of ll. 1118, 1119. It is a poor copy, full of blunders and corruptions, and of small value even for purposes of collation. A comparison of the readings of G., given on pp. 4-7, 10, with the corresponding readings in this MS., shows that it agrees with G. in ll. 960, 961, 1074, 1135, 1187, 1212 (of which it gives a corrupt form), 1235. In 928 it gives a new and unsupported reading. In ll. 1115, 1160, 1203, it agrees with, or nearly agrees with, only Pepys. In the remaining lines, it more or less agrees with one or another of the three MSS., F., R., A. In common with Pepys, it confirms G. in 1139. It resembles F.T.B. in 1107, 1269, 1296, 1355, 1357.

We must regard it, on the whole, as belonging to the group of MSS. showing revision, though it occupies a position nearer to G. than the other MSS. except Pepys. Its relationship to the Pepys MS. is evident on every page, and we must believe that the copies of the *Legend of Dido* in the two MSS. were to a great extent derived from the same corrupted source.

This MS. offers its own readings of two lines that are apparently corrupt in all the MSS. :—

1126 Thus gafe this honorable quene her gyftes all*e*.
1133 To her that all thise nobill thynges sent (P. *this* for *thise*).

MS., Ff. 1. 6. *in the Camb. Univ. Lib.* (*paper*).—This MS. contains only the *Legend of Thisbe*, omitting ll. 886, 898. It is a late and poor transcript. Its spelling is strange and careless, e.g. *owre* for *wre*, *attar* for *hotter*, *condyth* for *conduit*, *estwhard* for *estward*. The scribe is evidently ignorant of Chaucer's grammatical and metrical system, and, besides, seems occasionally unable to decipher the writing, or understand the sense, of his original: see the nonsense in ll. 788, 797-799, 885, 912.

In view of ll. 718, 780, 856, 887, it must be included among the MSS. showing a revised text of the legend. On the other hand, in 738 *cope* for *top*, 750 *that, that*, 794 *hast* for *lykyng*, 864 *therwith* for *therwithal*, 890 *my* for *thy*, 916 *his* (is?) for *ar*, it seems to betray affinities to a MS. of the G. type, for G. is the only MS. which shows *all* these readings.

Again, in ll. 765 *and eyke thy stone*, 907 *Than euer had pyramus and tesby*, we have readings which are peculiar to the F.T.B. group and γ., which is in some respects allied to them. Owing to the corrupt state of the text and its fragmentary character, it would be idle to speculate on its relationships.

Two of its readings are worthy of attention :—

837 *My bydyng hath you slayne in this case.* For *bydyng*, which is possibly correct, see p. 111.

903 *That in one graue we motton both lye.* This reading confirms A.

Wm. Thynne's edition of the "Legend of Good Women" (1532).—Thynne's text omits lines 960, 961, 1326, 1327, and not only gives 2338 in G.R.A. (with a variation), but also includes the spurious line (2339) found in F.T.B. and γ. He supplies all the lines, except 960, 961, that are missed in common by F.T.B.

The evidence supplied by the text shows that Thynne must have had several MSS. to work upon; that for the most part he followed, even in their defects, some MS. or MSS. of the F.T.B. type; and that occasionally he referred to MSS. of a different type. Some of this evidence will presently be given: more could be added, but the matter hardly merits the labour of an exhaustive analysis, for there is nothing even to suggest a suspicion that Thynne was in possession of a MS. of higher value than, or in any material respects different from, the MSS. that are extant, and that have been printed by the Chaucer Society. He gives numerous defective readings from some source, or sources, of the F.T.B. type of MSS., while he also occasionally indulges in random borrowings from other MSS., from which, in all probability, he could have obtained sounder readings. In other words, his text does not appear to be either a faithful copy of any one good MS., or a careful collation of different authorities. It may be added that he sometimes appears to offer readings of his own which are far from happy (see 1730, 1790, 1798, 2484, 2511).

In support of the statement that he followed some MS. or MSS. of the F.T.B. type, I would point (*inter alia*) to lines 196, 217, 555, 664, 907, 994, 1079, 1269, 1472, 1747, 1811, 1949, 2020, 2525. In 1056 and 1063 he gives readings which are found only in B. of the three MSS., though the latter reading is seen in γ. (*hadde* for *had*) as well. For some portion of the poem, he appears to follow T., or a duplicate of T., rather than F. or B.: see ll. 1369 *sleer deuourer*, 1536 *him had leauer* (also in R. and γ.), 1568 *on* for *of* (also in γ.),

1736 *heuynesse* for *honeste*, 1821 *and a very*, 1839 *the wo to tel were impossible*, 1850 *samples* for *ensamples*, 1888 *nat for thy sake onely written is this storie*, 1892 Th. *wrathe*, T. *wreth*, for *wreche*, 2480 *humbly*, T. *humble,* for *homely*.

On the other hand, he seems to follow a MS. of the R. or *a*. type in 40 (R.), 510 (*a*.), 533 (*a*.), 861 (*a*.R.), 1046 (R. only), 1085 (R. also G.γ.), 1143 (*a*.R.), 1635 (*a*. *fully* for *full*), 2044 (R.), 2265 (R.), 2452 (R. *quene Phillis*), 2501 (R. *your* for *oure* ; also G.).

In lines 831, 856, 1727 his readings are of the G. type. His readings in 249, 487, 846, 1490, 1643, 1998—some of the lines missed in common by F.T.B.—were possibly taken from the same source.

In lines 1172, 1798, 2338-2340, Thynne has combined the readings of the F.T.B. type with readings of other MSS.

Unsatisfactory Character of the MSS.

The question whether the different texts, or any one of them, can be held to represent an original embodying all the poet's emendations, and presenting an approved cast of the poem, demands consideration. For various reasons, the question appears to require an answer in the negative.

(1) All the MSS. presenting the revised version are full of corruptions, and betray signs of having been more or less edited.

(2) Not a few of the variations among the MSS. point to divergencies in the earliest copies of the poem in its revised form, *e.g.* the omission of lines 960, 961 in F.T.B.R.*a*.A.

(3) The variations of reading in respect to the lines which appear to have undergone revision seem to indicate that the scribes who were responsible for the earliest transcriptions were either uncertain as to the author's real intentions, or interpreted these intentions in different ways.

(4) All the MSS. showing the revised lines—except P. and Rl.— present spurious lines in place of 1139 in G. (*But natheles oure autour tellith vs*). This fact seems to indicate an intention on the part of the author to cancel this line, but it also suggests that the author's intended emendation was unknown to the scribes.

(5) The text in G. presents several blunders and defects. The texts

in the other MSS. exhibit the same blunders and defects, or present evidence of different individual attempts to get rid of these. *E.g.* :

1126 G. *Thus can this honurable quene here gestis calle.* This line is repeated in several of the MSS., and is somewhat modified in others, but in all it is a line of six measures. In all, except Rl., the meaning of the line is obscure.

1133 G. *To hȳ that alle thyngis hym sente.* There are several readings for this line in the other MSS. In F.T.B.A.α. the readings are bad. P.Rl. read, *To hir that alle this* (Rl. *thise*) *noble thynges sent*; but this reading is open to suspicion, as the texts in these MSS. are late, and in many ways unsatisfactory, and as, moreover, the reading eliminates the pronoun *him*, which occurs in all the other texts. R. reads, *To hyr that all thys nobyll thyng him sent*, and α. resembles this with *hym* for *hyr*.

1338 G.* *And seyde O swete cloth whil Iuppiter it leste.* This line of *six* measures is repeated in F.T.B.Th.P.γ.Rl., but is reduced to a line of *five* measures in R.α.A. by the omission of the word *swete*.

1339.* This line seems to show *six* measures in G. There are several different readings in the other MSS., of which some make no sense, and others are hypermetrical.

1936, 1964. In both these lines, G. reads *Theseus* where *Minos* is intended. The error had obviously been noticed, as the right name is substituted for Theseus in all the other MSS. In most cases, however, the verse is lame, as a dissyllable has taken the place of a trisyllable. The defect has in some way been remedied in respect to 1936 in R.α.A., and in respect to 1964 only in A.

1966. All the authorities—except R.α. and Th.—have the same error as G. in making *Athenes* the residence of Ariadne. In R.α.Th. various unsatisfactory alterations have been made in order to eliminate the error.

2422. The MSS. do not exhibit any recognition of the error in the *ghost*-name, *Thorus* (R. *Thora*). Thynne alters the word to *chorus*, having probably in view Virg. *Æn.* v. 823 *et sq.*

Unfortunately, no outside evidence exists which would enable us to understand the processes that were in operation in producing the divergencies among the MSS. that have just been illustrated. It is, however, possible to suggest a hypothesis which would account for the existence of many of these divergencies—viz., that some

* See p. 111.

of the extant MSS. are descended from copies made, not from the author's revised and finished draft of the poem (which, if such ever existed, was intended, in all probability, for presentation to the Court, and may have been inaccessible for purposes of transcription), but from a MS. containing what may be called Chaucer's working copy of the poem, on the pages of which the poet had entered his corrections, and proposed emendations for his own guidance. With such a copy of the poem to transcribe from, it is not improbable that a copyist might have experienced some difficulty in making up his mind as to the precise nature of the proposed insertions, omissions, or substitutions, indicated, perhaps not very clearly, in the margin or between the lines. Under such conditions, two copies made by the same scribe at different times might differ, and two copies made by different scribes would, not improbably, show divergent applications of the poet's corrections.

I suggest that G. is a descendant of Chaucer's draft of the poem before he had made his corrections and emendations, and that some of the other MSS. are descendants of copies of the poem made from his working copy, in which he entered such corrections and alterations as he may have thought necessary. This hypothesis has been suggested by many of the facts already indicated, and appears to find confirmation in other peculiarities, some of which I shall now illustrate.

1115 G. Ne stede for *to iuste* wel to gon. Here F.B.T.Th.R.A. *the Iustyng*, P. *the Iuste*, Rl. *the Iustes*, in place of *to iuste*. To the reading in G., which I suggest is the original reading, Chaucer perhaps took exception on the ground of the awkwardness of construction involved in the succession of infinitives. Let us accept the hypothesis that in his MS. *to* was corrected to *the*, and the various readings in the other MSS. can readily be accounted for.

1175. G. *ek thereto*; F.B.T., *withal*; R.A.a.P., *therewithal*. Here we may suppose that Chaucer scored out *ek* and *to* in his MS., and inserted *withal* in the margin or between the lines. His intention would appear to have been correctly understood in the case of the texts in R.A.a.P., and to have been misunderstood in respect to the text in F.T.B.

1370 G. *Of tendere wemen gentil cryaturys*. Here we may suppose that a line was drawn in the MS. from *tendere* to *gentil* in order to indicate that the words should be interchanged. Such an emendation would have been correctly interpreted in the reading *gentyl wemen tendre creatures* of R.a.A., and misinterpreted in the reading *gentil women gentil creatures* of F.T.B.γ.P.

In some instances, such as, perhaps, ll. 1139, 2338, the poet may have scored out words and cancelled whole lines without entering his proposed emendations.

I see nothing unreasonable in the hypothesis here suggested: on the other hand, it appears to offer an adequate basis for accounting for many of the peculiarities above mentioned, as well as for many of the divergencies in the readings of the MSS. Whatever may be the facts of the case, it is evident that no one of the extant MSS. of the *Legend of Good Women* can be said to represent the poet's finished and finally approved work.

The Order of the Legends.

There is a general agreement among the texts examined in respect to the order of the legends, and this fact affords a strong presumption that the order in which the legends have come down to us is the order which Chaucer gave to them. The order is presumably that in which they were written.

Summary of the Results obtained.

1. A comparison of the texts of the Prologue in the different MSS. confirms generally the deductions obtained from the examination of the texts of the legends. In particular, it is clear that G. is absolutely unique. The form of Prologue in F.T.B.R.a.A.P., and of the fragment in γ., is distinct from that in G.; but all these MSS., with the exception of a few minor differences, agree in the form of Prologue presented by them.

2. The legends down to and including the *Legend of Ariadne*, appear to have undergone revision at the hands of the poet. As there is no satisfactory evidence of revision after this legend, it may be presumed that the remaining legends were written after the issue of the earlier legends in their revised form.

3. G. presents an earlier draft of the legends. The other MSS. and Thynne's printed edition of 1532 present revised drafts of the legends or of fragments thereof.

4. G. is without doubt the oldest and least corrupted text, and possesses the highest authority among the surviving MSS. Next

in value to G. as authorities for the text are F.T.B., and, in spite of its fragmentary character, also γ., which is possibly a copy of a much older MS. R.α.A.β. possess considerable value for purposes of collation. Th.P.Rl. present texts of a composite or hybrid character and are of little value; with the Ff. fragment, they might be neglected, except for the purpose of consultation in the matter of disputed readings.

5. G. is unique, and the other MSS. may be thus classified according to their relationships :—*

(i.) P.Rl., (ii.) R.α., (iii.) Aβ., (iv.) γ., (v.) F.T.B.

The members of Group (i.) to some extent take up a position between G. and Groups (ii.) and (iii.). The members of Groups (ii.) and (iii.) seem to be related to one another, and occupy a position intermediate between G. and Group (v.). Taken as a whole, γ. occupies a position between Groups (ii.) and (iii.) on the one side and Group (v.) on the other. Thynne's edition is for the most part more closely related to Group (v.) (to T. in particular) than to the other groups.

A Critical Edition of the Legend.

In view of the results of the examination of the different texts, it is clear that there is no one MS. which would serve throughout as a satisfactory basis for a critical text of the legends. On the other hand, it has been shown that G. presents the best text for a large majority of the lines in the legends, and that, though its text appears to have undergone revision so far as Legends I.-VI. are concerned, the revision appears to have involved no organic or structural changes, but to have been almost confined to the modification of individual lines. In view of these circumstances, I am of opinion that, in the preparation of a critical text of the legends, it would be desirable—

(i.) in the main to base this text on G.;

(ii.) in the case of (a) all lines which appear to have undergone revision, (b) of all omissions in G., (c) of all unsound or defective

* I do not exhibit the relationships among the texts by means of a genealogical tree. In the case of some MSS., internal evidence appears to justify a conviction that they are descended from a common ancestor, but is inconclusive in respect to the determination of the number of transcriptions separating the common ancestor from the MSS. compared. Again, internal evidence sometimes suggests the view that a text is of a composite character, betraying obligations of varying extent to different MSS. In these circumstances, a genealogical tree could not adequately represent the relationships, and, if employed, would only mislead.

readings in G., to reconstruct a text based on a collation of the readings of F.T.B., after these have been checked with one another, of the readings of γ., and of the readings of R.a. and of A.β. after the members of each of these groups have been checked with one another;

(iii.) in all doubtful cases to reproduce the readings of G., unless these are obviously unsound.

For a critical edition of the Prologue, it would, I think, be advisable to print the two versions side by side. The revised version should be based mainly on a collation of F.T.B.; but all material variations between the readings of these MSS. and the readings of R.a.A. should be carefully indicated. Very many of the lines of the Prologue in the G. version have been retained in the revised version.

Such an edition, without doubt, would in many respects be imperfect, but it would, I believe, present a fair approximation to Chaucer's work.

Part II.—The Prologues to the "Legend of Good Women."

Section I.—Which Version of the Prologue is the earlier?

Which of the two forms of Prologue is the earlier is a question that will now be considered.* Attention will first be drawn to the differences in readings of individual lines, as distinct from the differences in spirit and in arrangement, and also from such differences as arise from excisions or insertions. When these differences in readings are compared, it is at once obvious that the author

* This question has been discussed by several writers. B. ten Brink (*Englische Stud.*, xvii., pp. 13-23) was of opinion that G. presented the later or revised version of the Prologue, and his views seem to be shared by Dr. Köppel (*Englische Stud.*, xvii., p. 196), and Dr. Kaluza (*Englische Stud.*, xxii., p. 281). On the other hand, Dr. F. J. Furnivall (*Trial Forewords*, 104-7), and Prof. W. W. Skeat (*Chaucer's Works*, III., pp. 22-5) hold the view that G. presents the Prologue in an earlier form, while Dr. John Koch (*The Chronology of Chaucer's Writings*, Chaucer Soc. Sec., Ser. 27, Appendix), and Prof. Emile Legouis ("*Quel fut le premier composé . . . des deux Prologues de la Légende des femmes exemplaires?*") have attacked the position taken up by the learned ten Brink. My examination of the question was completed before I became acquainted with the views of Dr. Köppel and Dr. Kaluza on the one side, or of Prof. E. Legouis on the other. In certain respects, my own discussion resembles the essay of the latter scholar, and I may add that the resemblances might have been even closer had I not determined to abstain as much as possible from arguments on the æsthetic side which would appeal with varying degrees of force to different minds. I cordially endorse the statement of Prof. Legouis, that the B. text (*i.e.* the text as it stands in F.) "offre des marques évidentes de progrès; il est plus plein, plus harmonieux, plus beau; il est litterairement plus parfait." I owe it to myself to add that my argument stands as it did before I became acquainted with the graceful essay of Prof. Legouis.

has revised his readings, those in G. being in every case compared inferior to the readings presented by the other MSS.

I proceed to cite the readings that indicate revision, and shall classify them into the following groups for the sake of convenience:—

i. changes involving an improvement in logic or the structure of sentences;

ii. changes involving the introduction or modification of alliterative effects;

iii. changes involving the elimination of unpleasant assonances;

iv. changes involving the elimination of an additional syllable other than a light *e* final before the cesural pause.

N.B.—For this examination the readings of G. will for the most part be compared with those of F., which may be taken as typical of the other MSS., so far as the Prologue is concerned.

 i. *Improvements in logic and the structure of sentences.*

12, 13, 14 G. Men schal nat wenyn euery thyng alye
     ffor that he say it nat of yore a-go
     God wot a thyng is neuere the lesse so.
   F. Men shal not wenen euery thyng a lye
     But yf him-selfe yt seeth or elles dooth
     For God wot thing is neuer the lasse sooth.

Here the argument is more comprehensive, and in line 14 hypotaxis replaces parataxis.

21. G. and trowyn on . . . F. that tellen of.
 Construction rendered more compact.

27, 28 G. Wel oughte vs thanne on olde bokys leue
    There as there is non othyr a-say be preue.
   F. Wel ought vs thanne honouren and beleve
    These bokes there we han noon other preve.
More logically expressed.

31, 32 G.; 32, 31 F. More logically expressed.

39 G. ffarwel myn stodye as lastynge that sesoun.
  F. Faire-wel my boke and my deuocion.

The attractions of May are more vigorously expressed; they are stronger than books or religion.

84 G.; 100 F. More logically expressed.

 ⎰ 116, 117 G. Now hadde the tempre sonne al that releuyd
 ⎱   And clothede hym in grene al newe a-geyn.
 ⎰ 128, 129 F. Now hath thatempre sonne all that releued
 ⎱   That naked was and clad yt new agayn.

Clearer and more compact in structure.

126-128 G.; 138-140 F. More clearly expressed.
163-166 G.; 232-234 F. More briefly expressed, and contradictory hyperbole eliminated.
222 G. *ne pleyne* is inconsistent with the context and is altered to *ye tweyne* in line 268 of the other MSS.

{ 234 G. I lenynge faste by vndyr a bente.
{ 308 F. I knelyng by this floure in good entente.

Greater appropriateness in the description. The poet brings himself out into the open, and, instead of reclining, adopts the more respectful attitude of one kneeling.

238 G.; 312 F. See 234 G.; 308 F. above.

242, 244 G.; 316, 318 F. More logical; the poet had come to see the daisy, and was not guilty of audacity in approaching the god of love.

{ 254 G. It nedeth nat to glose   }
{ 328 F. Withouten nede of glose   } Improved construction.

323-327 G.; 347-349 F. The modifications are more consistent with the dignity of a god.

{ 330-332 G. That tabourryn in youre eres manye a thyng
{   ffor hate or for Ielous ymagynyng
{   And for to han with you sum dalyaunce.
{ 354-356 F. That tabouren in your eres many a swon
{   Ryght aftir hire ymagynacion
{   To have youre daliance and for envie.

Improvement in logical arrangement of ideas.

348 G. This line, which appears to have no logical connexion with the context, is replaced by another (368 F.) that has.

509 G., *and ek*; 521 F., *and in.* Construction balanced.

ii. *The introduction or modification of alliterative effects.**

1	G. sythis (thousent, telle)		F. tymes
32	G. swich lust and swich	31	F. I feyth and ful
149	G. mane flourys (schal)	217	R.A. flowres smale
228	G. sat, thanne this	302	F. sat, syth his
248	G. myn mortal fo and me	322	F. my foo and al my folke

iii. *Removal of unpleasant assonances or repetitions.*

21 G. trow*yn on*   21 F. tell*en of*
28 G. there as there is. *Line recast*

* In neither the Prologue nor the legends have I noticed any sacrifice of alliterative effects in the revised lines.

29	G. Myn wit be lite.	29	F. I konne but lyte
39	G. *Excessive sibilancy eliminated*		
40	G. therto this	40	R. then eke thys (F.B. suche a,
84	G. There as there lyth. *Line recast*		T. thanne ek)
228	G. thanne this	302	F. syth his (R.A.*a*.P̂. the)
231	G. degre (unpleasant inner rime with *they*)	305	F. estaat
343	G. and takyth non hed of what matere he take	365	F. Hym rekketh noght of what matere he take

iv. *Elimination of additional syllable at the cesural pause.*

5	G. that dwellyth (?)	5	F. duellyng (?)
35	G. other vp-on	35	F. seldom on
39	G. ffarwel myn stodye as lastynge that scsoun		
39	F. Faire-wel my boke and my deuocion		
48	G. these flouris	48	F. this floure
320	G. Ageyns these poyntys		that ye han to hym mevid
344	F. Agyns al this		
411	G. That hightyn baladis roundelys and vyrelayes		
423	F. That highten balades roundels virelayes		
436	G. To me ne fond I neuere non betere than the		
446	F. To me ne founde y better noon than yee		
451	G. That han me holpyn and put me in swich degre		
461	F.T. That han me holpe and put me (R.A.B.*a*. om. *me*) in this degree
483	G. That he schal charge hise seruauntys by ony weye (F.T.B. Th.A.P. = G.)
493	R.*a*. That he hys seruantes charge by eny way

Moreover, the following lines in G., which present what may be an extra syllable at the pause other than a light *e* final, have nothing corresponding to them in the other drafts of the Prologue ; 54, *morwe* ; 91, *medewe* ; 107, *medewe* ; 143, *comyth* (comth ?) ; 271, *bokys* ; 280, *Valerye* ; 316, *repente it* ; 360, *owith* ; 362, *heryn* ; 414 (reading doubtful).

On the other hand, extra syllables other than a light *e* final which occur in G. also occur in the other MSS. in lines G. 62, F. 74, *ropyn* ; G. 155, F. 223, *coroun* ; G. 255, R.A. 329, *translated* ; G. 358, F. 378, *fermour*. In G. 373, F. 387 :—*ffor they ben half goddys in this world(e) here*—" half-goddys " is probably a compound, and, as the accent falls on the first member, is dissyllabic.

Also extra syllables at the pause other than *e* final, though not occurring in G., are perhaps to be found in the other MSS. in lines

Chaucer's Legend of Good Women

13, *seeth*; 37, *comen*; 98, *olde stories*; 115, *knees*; 150, *diden* (dide?); 196, *olde story*; 255, *comith*; 262, *comith*; 269, *cometh*. However, in lines 13, 115, 255, 262, 269, the words indicated may be monosyllabic; and in 98, *olde stories* should perhaps be *stories olde*, as G. reads (82) *bokys olde*. Besides the examples just enumerated, F.T.B. show an extra syllable in lines 89 (*werkes*), 399 (*reward vnto*), but these readings are not supported by R.a.A.P.

As in the above lists we have numerous specific examples of undeniable improvements upon the readings in G., and as against these very little can be brought forward on the other side, we must conclude that in the Prologue, as in the legends, G. represents an earlier draft of the poem, and that the other MSS. represent revised drafts.

This inference is supported by other considerations, some of which will now be mentioned.

The two forms of the Prologue are clearly distinguished from one another by the difference of the spirit or the tone that characterises them. In the G. version there is no special laudation of the queen, while the language employed by the poet in dealing with the duties of a king is admonitory, and even almost minatory (see lines 368-9). In the other version, there is an unmistakable note of gratitude and loyalty to the queen, while the lecture on the duties of a king, as will be shown later, breathes a different spirit. Now it is impossible to accept the suggestion that the G. version was the later of the two versions,[*] and that, owing to loss of favour at Court, Chaucer deliberately excised the passages eulogising the queen. It is true that the later recensions of Gower's *Confessio Amantis*, in which the eulogy of King Richard occurring in an earlier text seems to have been excised, afford what at first sight may be regarded as a case in point that may be cited in support of this view. But as Mr. G. C. Macaulay[†] has shown, Gower's *Confessio Amantis* was not dedicated to the king, but to the Earl of Derby, afterwards Henry IV., and there is no evidence to justify the view that Gower was a timeserver. Whatever Gower may have been, it is impossible to believe that Chaucer could have turned his back on the king or queen, for the evidence of state-records makes it extremely probable that he was high in favour with the Court up to the middle of 1391, when he

---

[*] Of the learned ten Brink. What follows is suggested by one of his statements. See *Englische Stud.*, xvii., pp. 13 ff.

[†] Works of John Gower, II., pp. xxiii. to xxviii.

lost his appointment of Clerk of the Works in connexion with certain royal palaces and other buildings.* What caused the loss of this appointment cannot be stated, but we do know that, early in 1394, he received a pension for life from the king; that he occasionally received advances on his pension; and that, in 1398, he obtained letters of protection from the king.* These facts do not point to any loss of Court favour, and afford no justification for the view that Chaucer was guilty of an attempt at petty revenge. In view of these considerations, the aforesaid position would appear to be untenable. On the other hand, it would be quite natural that Chaucer should have added a good deal of new eulogistic matter if, after writing his first draft of the Prologue, he had received new favours at the hands of the sovereign or his consort. That this is probably the correct view of the case will presently be shown in Section iv.

Again, there is something to be said in respect to the change in some of the features of the dream-fable, and also in the plan of the poem.

In the G. version of the Prologue, though the *balade* is sung in honour of Alcestis, and its refrain announces her presence, the poet does not recognise her till the god of love informs him of her identity (487-506). Moreover, the *balade*, somewhat incongruously, is sung by the assembly of women, among whom, presumably, are the very ladies named therein. These remarkable inconsistencies are absent in the other form of the Prologue, in which the poet himself introduces the *balade* and seems to dedicate it to his "lady souereyne," and not explicitly to Alcestis. This circumstance points to revision, but, on the other hand, the poet would appear to have overlooked line 422 in G., as the line is reproduced in the other version (see 432), and introduces the name of Alcestis prematurely.

In the G. version, the scheme of the poem apparently contemplated an indefinite number of legends; in the other version, it would appear that the number was to be limited.† Now, whether the composition of the legend was a set task which the poet was commanded to perform, or a piece of work voluntarily undertaken in honour of the queen, it is impossible to believe, more especially in view of his language in the *Legend of Phyllis* (2454-7), that the less ambitious and less laborious scheme was expanded into a larger and a heavier

* Dr. F. J. Furnivall, *Trial Forewords*, pp. 21 ff
† This matter is discussed in Section iii.

one. It is much more probable that the larger scheme underwent some curtailment, especially as the poet must about this time have been engaged on his Canterbury Tales.

Finally, much might be said in reference to the passages that occur in one and are absent in the other of the versions of the Prologue. Some of these passages will be dealt with for a different purpose in another section of this dissertation, and I shall here call attention only to the long passage in G.—lines 267-312—to which there is nothing corresponding in the other version. This passage, which approaches dangerously near to the pedantic, is in great measure autobiographical in character. It is true that Chaucer puts all the details concerning his library and the learned works with which he was familiar into the mouth of the God of Love, who, in virtue of his godhead, may be supposed to have a knowledge of everything; but the passage is autobiographical, nevertheless, and to me seems somewhat out of place in its setting. That such a passage should have been omitted is more consistent with the theory of revision than that it should have been interpolated. Further, I would suggest that its omission may in part have depended on the restriction of the plan of his poem already referred to, for, with fewer legends to write, it was not necessary for him to ransack whole libraries.

In the light of these considerations, it must be held that G. presents an earlier draft of the Prologue, as well as an earlier draft of the legends or of some of them.

Before proceeding to discuss the question of the dates at which the Prologues were composed, I propose to deal with (1) the circumstances out of which the *Legend of Good Women* arose, (2) the plan of the poem.

Section ii.—The Circumstances out of which the Legend arose.

There can be little doubt that the Legend was undertaken by Chaucer at the express request—by the command, as it would be now described—of Queen Anne, or of King Richard at the instigation of his queen. This position, if not absolutely demonstrable as a proposition, can be sustained by arguments that, in the circumstances, might be fairly called convincing, and that, at any rate, are far stronger than many which find acceptance in the discussion of similar questions.

First, to direct attention to *explicit* evidence. In lines 496, 497 of the revised version of the Prologue, we have the statement that the Legend, when "*made*," was *to be presented on behalf of Alcestis to the queen at Eltham or at Sheen*. Now, one of the most characteristic features which distinguish the revised from the earlier version is that, while the latter presents the fable more or less consistently as a dream throughout—even to the last lines—in the former Chaucer seems frequently to forget the conditions of a dream-fable, and lapses from the dreamer into the man awake and in contact with the solid realities of life. The passage under reference is of the kind described, and it can mean only that the work, when completed, was to be presented to Queen Anne at one of the two royal residences indicated. The queen referred to could not be Richard's second queen, whom he married in 1396, for the latter was a mere child, to whom such language as Chaucer employs could not be applied. Moreover, Stow * informs us that, after cursing the place where Anne died (*i.e.* Sheen), Richard "did also for anger throw down the buildings." The passage, therefore, must be taken as providing a specific statement that the poem was intended for Queen Anne.

It is true that the passage under consideration does not occur in the earlier draft of the Prologue, but, as the main features of the fable in the two forms of the Prologue are identical, and as both forms describe the Legend as a penance enjoined on the poet at the suggestion of the same individual, we may feel sure that in the earlier, as in the later version, Anne was to be identified with Alcestis.

The foregoing evidence is supported by the statement of Lydgate, who, in his Prologue to the *Fall of Princes*, says of Chaucer:—

> The poete wrote at the request of the quene
> A Legende of perfite holynesse
> Of Good Women.

Though we are not in a position to define the nature of Lydgate's personal relations to Chaucer, or to take for granted that his statement in respect to the Legend is based on any authoritative information at his disposal, his evidence nevertheless possesses some

* *Annales* (1615), p. 309, col. 2.

Chaucer's Legend of Good Women

value as embodying his own or current opinion on the matter at a time not very distant from the date of the composition of the Legend.

Lydgate's evidence, taken with what has gone before, justifies the inference that Queen Anne was the inspiring source of the poem. There is other evidence, which, though not explicit in character, possesses considerable value in confirming this inference. There are many statements in the Prologue which, forming part of the texture of the dream-fable, present but a thin veil of symbolisation through which it is easy to distinguish the outlines of solid underlying fact. In the description of the God of Love and of Alcestis, we cannot fail to recognise allusions to the king and queen.

That Alcestis represents the queen is clear from the revised version of the Prologue. In lines 241–276, which include the *balade*, it is to be observed that Chaucer employs language which is more applicable to the lady of his devotion than to Alcestis. More particularly is it worthy of notice that, while in line 248 the *balade* is dedicated to "this lady fre," *i.e.* the "noble quene" of line 241, who turns out to be Alcestis, in lines 270–275 he justifies the introduction of the *balade* by saying that it is applicable to his "lady souereyne," an expression which, neither literally nor metaphorically, can be regarded as an appropriate description of the relations of Alcestis to the poet. Again, in lines 82–93 of the revised version, the daisy, which in the fable symbolises Alcestis, is described as the flower which the poet both *loves* and *dreads*, and to which he is ever ready to render obedient service. Here, again, the poet's meaning, if his language is applied only to the daisy or to Alcestis, is far from clear. On the other hand, everything becomes intelligible if we assume that the poet intends both daisy and Alcestis to serve but as a veil to the identity of good Queen Anne. It is hardly necessary to dilate on the emphasis that is placed on the benignity of Alcestis (G. 175, 179, F. 243, 276)—a quality of heart which, as is well known, was one of Anne's most striking characteristics.*

That the God of Love was intended to symbolise the king is

---

* In the letter of attorney (26th December, 1380) given to the English Commissioners to negotiate his marriage with Anne, King Richard says that he chose her "*nedum propter ipsius nobilitatem, set propter Famam celebrem bonitatis ipsius, nostris auribus instillatam.*"—Rymer's *Fœdera*.

a hypothesis which derives some confirmation from the following passages :—

G. 158–164. I-clothede was this myghty god of loue
Of silk I-broudede ful of grene greuys
A garlond on his hed of rose leuys
Stekid al with lylye flourys newe
But of his face I can not seyn the hewe
ffor sekyrly his face schon so bryhte
That with the glem a-stonede was the syhte.

F. 226–232. Y-clothed was this myghty god of love
In silke enbrouded ful of grene greves
In with a fret of rede rose leves
The fresshest syn the worlde was first bygonne
His gilte here was corowned with a sonne
I-stede of golde for heuynesse and wyght
Therwith me thoght his face shoon so bryght.

Parable-reading, though full of attractions, has its limitations and dangers, so that great caution is necessary on the part of the interpreter. On the other hand, as allegory springs out of a desire to give a vagueness to what is real and substantial, by means of the methods of allusion or suggestion, it is but natural that, when an allegory offers itself to our notice, we should expect to discover its inner meaning by means of the surrounding allusions or suggestions. It happens that, in the particular passages above cited, there appear to be definite allusions to known facts.

(1) There seems to be an obvious reference to Richard's beauty of face and his auburn or golden hair. [See the *diptych** in Wilton House, the seat of the Earl of Pembroke, or the copy of this portrait of the king in Shaw's *Dresses and Decorations of the Middle Ages*; the portrait of Richard II. in Westminster Abbey; the portrait of Richard II. belonging to the Earl of Scarborough, the frame of which bears the date 1384, and which, according to Planché (*Jour. Brit. Arch. Assoc.*, xxii. p. 36), is a close imitation of the celebrated original portrait in Westminster Abbey; also Dean Stanley (*Memorials of Westminster Abbey*, p. 124); and Richard de Maidstone (*Richard's Reconciliation with the City of London*, 1393) in Wright's *Political Poems and Songs*, vol. i., p. 285.]

(2) In the statement in the earlier version that the garland was

---

* The date of this is stated to be 1377, at which time Richard was only ten or eleven years of age, but the face and figure are rather those of a youth of fifteen or sixteen.

"stekid with lylye flourys newe," there seems to be a reference to the recently-advanced claim * of the English kings to the crown of France, a claim which was heraldically represented in the quartering of the *lilies* in the escutcheons of Edward III., the Black Prince, and Richard II. (Sandford, *Genealogical History of the Kings and Queens of England*, Bk. III., chap. iii. 157; chap. iv. 185; chap. v. 191).

(3) In both versions, the robe of silk worn by the God of Love is described as being ornamented with *grene greves*. Now, as *greves* may here mean "twigs," or "sprays" (see *Knightes Tale*, 649, 650), there seems to be a reference to what was one of Richard's favourite devices. In the Wilton House picture above referred to, he is represented as wearing a rich red robe embroidered with the crowned hart *in circles of vetch beans* (see the copy of the picture in Shaw's *Dresses and Decorations of the Middle Ages*). He "used also a peascod branch, with the cods open but the peas out, as it is upon his robe in his monument of Westminster" (Sandford, *Gen. Hist. of the Kings and Queens of Eng.*, Bk. III., chap. v., p. 191). A beautiful set of drawings of the effigies of Richard and Anne in Westminster Abbey will be found in *Monumental Effigies of Great Britain*, by Thomas and George Hollis, in which the *peascod branch*, the *broom plant*, and other devices, are clearly represented.

(4) In lines 230, 231 of the revised version, a *sonne* takes the place of the garland in the earlier version. It happens that a sun emerging from behind a cloud was one of Richard's royal devices, as may be seen on his effigy in Westminster Abbey (see Hollis, *Monumental Effigies in Great Brit.*). This device seems to have been borrowed from his father, the Black Prince, and is, I think, referred to by Gower in his eulogy of the king in the *Confessio Amantis*.†

I submit that the significance of these various statements is unmistakable. In themselves, and without any other key to the explanation of the allegory, they afford but uncertain and inadequate ground on which to base a solution; but, taken in connection with the independent evidence which shows that the poet was writing at the request of the queen, they afford confirmation of this evidence.

So far we have been treading on what might be regarded as

* See also p. 103 below.
† Lich to the sonne in his degre
  Which with the cloudes up alofte
  Is derked and beshadewed ofte.—Pauli's edn., III., p. 376.

solid ground in the interpretation of the allegory, but there is some justification in going a little further in our inferences. We may well believe that, underlying Chaucer's statements in respect to the origin of the poem, there is a basis of fact. He seems to imply that he had been commanded to write a Legend of Good Women, that he was to work at this Legend (see G. 469-484)* every year to the end of his life, and that the queen had undertaken to request the king to command his servants to assist him in his work and compensate him for his labours. In other words, it would appear that Chaucer was called upon to give the Court a *quid pro quo* † in respect to the remuneration or favours he had received or was to receive, and that, in the Legend, we have, perhaps, the earliest example in the English language of a set annual task assigned to a Court poet, resembling in some respects the set task demanded from the Poet Laureate of a later age.

That the composition of the Legend was a *commanded*, and not a *self-imposed*, task may be inferred from the poet's language in the Legend of Phyllis (2454-2457) :—

> But for I am agroted heer-biforn
> To wryte of hem that been in love forsworn
> And eek to haste me in my legende
> Which to performe God me grace sende ; ‡

and again in 2490 :—

> Me list nat vouche-sauf on him to swinke.‡

Here such expressions as *agroted, performe, swinke*, suggest the impression that he regarded the work as no grateful task, and, even if

---

* I here follow the earlier version, and shall at a later point discuss the changes in the revised version.

† On 17th February, 1385, Chaucer obtained permission to appoint a deputy to perform the duties of his office of Comptroller of the Customs of Wools. We may conjecture that one of his reasons for seeking a relief from these duties was to obtain greater leisure for the prosecution of his literary work, and it may be presumed that, tacked on to the concession he now obtained, was a condition that he should execute some special work for the queen. It would appear as if, in a spirit of mischief and fun, she prescribed for him the task of producing an antidote to his translation of the *Romance of the Rose* and his *Troilus and Cressida*. If such instructions were issued in February, 1385, possibly the first instalment of his contribution is represented in the Prologue and the *Legend of Cleopatra*, which, as I shall endeavour to show, were probably written for the month of May in the same year.

‡ Quoted from works of G. Chaucer—ed. W. W. Skeat.

we look upon these passages as embodying good-humoured chaff at his own expense, it must be remembered that a good deal of serious earnestness frequently underlies Chaucer's gamesomeness. Moreover, it may be urged that the scheme of the Legend, as a whole, was one which could hardly have commended itself to the author's artistic temperament, and which it is improbable he would have voluntarily undertaken, in view of the burdensome monotony incidental to the treatment of such a subject. It is, perhaps, significant that he introduces into the Prologue of the Legend an apology for the choice of certain subjects in some of his poems, for the lines—

Or hym was bodyn make thilke tweye
Of sum persone and durste it not with-seye (G. 346, 347)

may have a wider application than at first sight they seem to bear.

If the task was one which Chaucer was commanded to perform, and which he was expected to proceed with *year by year* (G. 471-2, F. 481-2), then, in order to claim reward for his labour, presumably the poet would have had to give some proof of fresh work on the Legend performed every year or so. There is nothing unreasonable in the presumption that he may have contributed not less than one legend in the year. (See Bech, *Anglia*, V., 379, 380.) This presumption is not inconsistent with the known facts of Chaucer's life and work: on the other hand, it is consistent with ascertained facts, or what may be accepted as legitimate inferences from such facts.

In the first place, on the assumption that the poem was first undertaken in 1385 (arguments in support of this view will be advanced), there is an approximate correspondence between the number of legends and the number of years after the above date during which Queen Anne lived. A poem written by her orders, and in compliment to her, could not have been continued after her death, which occurred on the 7th June, 1394. From 1385 to 1394 we have a period of *ten* years. There are *ten* good women whose stories are given in *nine* legends. The coincidence in number may be accidental: it is at least consistent with the hypothesis. Further, I shall endeavour to show at a later stage of this discussion that the Second Prologue was written in 1390, or after an interval of *five* years after the First Prologue and the *Legend of Cleopatra* were written. I have already shown in an earlier part of this dissertation that we have evidence of a revision of the Legends up to and including the *Legend of Ariadne*, which is the *sixth* in order. As it seems fair to conjecture that the Legends were revised at the same time as the Prologue, we have another coincidence in numbers in which there is possibly some confirmation of the hypothesis now under consideration.

In the second place, as shown by me in *Notes and Queries* —8th S., IX., Ap. 18, 1896—there is good reason for supposing that the poem of *Anelida and Arcite* has some reference to the attempt of Robert de Vere, Earl of Oxford and Duke of Ireland, to obtain a divorce from his wife in order that he might be free to marry a Bohemian lady in the court of Queen Anne. As the Duke of Ireland effected his object early in 1387, the poem might have been written towards the close of 1386. Now Anelida's *Complaint*, in its leading motive, in its dramatic presentation of the play and transition of feelings and states of mind, and in some of the ideas and expressions employed, recalls Dido's letter to Encas in Ovid's *Heroides* (7th epist.), and I may add that the resemblance between these poems would appear to have been noticed as early as the 15th century, for in Shirley's MSS—Addit. 16,165, Brit. Mus., and Trin. Coll., Camb., R. 3.20—the *Complaint* is introduced as that of "Anelyda, Qweene of *Cartage.*" Now, as at the time Chaucer was occupied with the fate of Dido, it seems probable that, if he was also at work on the *Legend of Good Women*, he would have selected her story for one of the Legends. It is perhaps significant that the *Legend of Dido* is *third* in the order of the Legends, for, on the hypothesis suggested above, he would have been writing it about 1387.

Again, in the fact that Queen Anne was born in May (see *Dict. Nation. Biog.*—Anne), we may find the explanation of Chaucer's selection of a May scene as a background for the figures of his dream-picture. His statement that the month of May always draws him out of his bed and away from his studies and devotions to observe the *resurrection* of the daisy (see lines 36-49, and also 110 in the revised version) may be a symbolical way of describing something of the nature of an annual birthday tribute to the queen. That the Prologue in its earlier form was intended to commemorate the queen's birthday is a hypothesis that finds some confirmation in the selection of *nineteen* as the number of the ladies following the God of Love and Alcestis, and also as the number of women specially selected for commemoration in the *balade*, inasmuch as the queen, who was born in 1366, would have been nineteen years of age in 1385.

I submit that the cumulative effect of these various considerations is to give something more than a mere colour of probability to the hypothesis that the poet was expected to contribute at least one legend every year.

Section iii.—The Plan of the "Legend of Good Women."

I shall now consider the question of the contemplated plan of the *Legend of Good Women*. It is important to observe the difference in the language of the two versions of the Prologue. These agree in the following:—

G. 471-474.   Thow schalt whil thow leuyst yer be yere
              The moste partye of thyn lyf spende
              In makynge of a gloryous legende
              Of goode wemen maydenys and wyues.

F. 481-484.   Thow shalt while that thou lyvest yere by yere,
              The most partye of thy tyme spende
              In makyng of a glorious legende
              Of good wymmen, maydenes, and wyves.

They also agree in the instructions (1) that the legend was to begin with Cleopatra (see G. 542, F. 566), and (2) that the *Legend of Alcestis* was to be introduced after he had written the legends of other less important characters* (see G. 538-540, F. 548-550). There is no other suggestion in G. as to the plan to be followed than what is stated in the passages quoted or referred to above. If other lines on the subject existed in the original draft of the poem, they must either have been cancelled by the author or have been omitted during transcription. As the text stands in G., it would appear that the poet was commanded to continue writing all his life, and no limitation appears to be placed on the number of tales that he was to tell.

On the other hand, in lines 554-560 of the second form of the Prologue, we note a new instruction:—

> Thise other ladies sittynge here arowe
> Ben in thy (F. my) balade yf thou kanst hem knowe
> And in thy bookes alle thou shalt hem fynde
> Haue hem in thy legende now al in mynde
> I mene of hem that ben in thy knowyng
> For here ben twenty thousande moo sittyng
> Thanne thou knowest.

* There is no evidence in G. to show that the poem was to *end* with the *Legend of Alcestis*.

The language here is certainly not free from obscurity, more especially in view of line 558, in which Chaucer may be reserving to himself some freedom of selection, and also in view of the fact that, if the "other ladies sittynge here arowe" are the *nineteen* ladies attendant on the God of Love and the queen who accompanies him (G. 186, F. 283), only *eighteen* ladies are named in the revised form of the *balade*.* There is no authority in the G. Prologue for the opinion that the number of legends was to be restricted to *nineteen* or *twenty*. Line 554 of the revised Prologue affords a presumption that there were to be *nineteen* legends, and line 557 that the subjects of these legends were to be the ladies mentioned in the *balade*, who, with Alcestis, make up the number *nineteen*. In the list of works enumerated in the Retractation at the end of some copies of the *Canterbury Tales*, the *Legend of Good Women* is apparently referred to as "the book of the five-and-twenty ladies." As adjectives of number were often expressed by their equivalents in Roman numerals, it is possible that some error has crept into the text, xxv. having perhaps been written for another number. In any case, the passage in the Retractation cannot be adduced as evidence as to Chaucer's intentions in respect to the number of the legends. The view that Chaucer's plan or commission contemplated the incorporation of only *nineteen* legends derives considerable support from the almost contemporary testimony of Lydgate who, in the Prologue to his *Fall of Princes*, says that Chaucer wrote—

> A Legend of perfite holynesse
> Of Good Women to fynd out nynetene,

and proceeds to offer a humorous explanation of the poet's failing to complete the design.† That the plan was to be in some way limited

---

* In the original form of the *balade* we have the names of *nineteen* ladies, but one of these is Alcestis.

† What good women it was the poet's intention to select as the subjects of his legends is a question which has been discussed by several writers. Bech (*Anglia*, v., pp. 371-6) finds an answer to the question in the list given in the *balade*, and would appear to attach little importance to the list of ladies in the Prologue to the *Tale of the Man of Law*. B. ten Brink (*Englische Studien*, xvii., pp. 18, 19), and Prof. Skeat (*Works of G. Chaucer*, III., pp. xxv.–xxvii.) are disposed to arrive at a solution by a comparison of the two lists. With the greatest deference to the opinions of these learned writers, I feel bound to express the opinion that any attempt to solve the question must for the present be futile. Though we may legitimately infer that the plan of the L.G.W. was occupying the poet's thoughts at the time he was engaged on the Prologue to the *Tale of*

to a definite number of legends is an inference that seems legitimately to follow from lines 496, 497 of the revised version, in which he is told that *when this book ys made* he is to present it to the queen at Eltham or at Sheen.

If, then, we may assume that the G. text presents neither more nor less than the original form of the Prologue, we must conclude, lines 481, 482 in the revised form notwithstanding, that there was a change in the plan of the poem, and that Chaucer had at some time obtained permission to shorten his task.

Section iv.—The Date of Composition of the Legend.

As the *House of Fame* is mentioned in the Prologue to the *Legend of Good Women* (G. 405, F. 417), and as there is some reason for supposing that the former was commenced towards the end of 1383, and written before February, 1385,* we may infer that the latter cannot be assigned to an earlier date than 1384. Further, the Legend cannot be assigned to a later date than 1394, for on the 7th June of that year Queen Anne died of the pestilence at Sheen.

There are certain considerations which, I submit, justify us in fixing a more precise date. B. ten Brink (*Hist. Eng. Lit.*, Bk. IV. sec. 10), Dr. F. J. Furnivall (*Trial Forewords*), and Prof. Lounsbury

the Man of Law, we cannot accept the list therein given as affording an explicit statement of his intentions, as only *sixteen* ladies, including Canace, but excluding Alcestis and the daughter of Antiochus, are mentioned; while the list omits the names of Cleopatra and Philomela, whose legends are extant. On the other hand, too much weight should not be attached to the list in the *balade*, and to the statement in the lines 554-5 of the revised Prologue:—

"Thise other ladies sittynge here arowe,
Ben in thy balade yf thou kanst hem knowe."

If the "other ladies" are taken to refer to the "ladyes nyntene" of line 283, we are met with the difficulty that only *eighteen* ladies are mentioned in the *balade*, and that among these we do not find the names of Medea and Philomela, whose legends survive. It would almost appear as if Chaucer wished to give to his plans a vagueness in keeping with the character of his dream-picture.

Whether Lydgate's statement is based on facts known to him, or only embodies his interpretation of lines 554-558, cannot be determined. His testimony is valuable as representing early and almost contemporary opinion on the subject. The same opinion seems to find expression in the *Court of Love* (103-109), in which there are obvious references to the L.G.W., and *nineteen* is given as the number of "ladies gode."

* See Skeat (III., pp. xvi.-xix. and p. 248, note 111), who follows ten Brink (*Chaucer. Studien*).

(*Studies in Chaucer*, Vol. I., pp. 417, 418) seem to be of opinion that the composition of the Legend extended over a considerable period of time. In the foregoing discussion, I have offered some reasons for believing that such was the case, and I shall now go further, and endeavour to show that a period of about *five* years separated the dates of composition of the two Prologues.

Prof. Skeat (*Works of G. Chaucer*, III., pp. xix., xx.) fixes 1385 as the date of the composition of the Legend, on the ground that " the extremely grateful way in which Chaucer speaks of the queen may fairly be connected with the stroke of good fortune which happened to him just at this very period," in the indulgence—obtained on the 17th February, 1385—of being allowed to nominate a permanent deputy for his Comptrollership of the Customs and Subsidies, by means of which he was able to secure greater leisure. There can be no doubt that the poet does express himself in terms which betray a deep sense of gratitude to the queen for favours shown to him, but this description of Chaucer's feelings is applicable rather to his language in the revised form of the Prologue than to the language of the earlier version. I accept 1385 as the date for the earlier Prologue for reasons which, so far as I know, have never before been advanced.

There can be no doubt that, in the lecture on the duties of a king which Chaucer puts into the mouth of Alcestis, he is taking advantage of Queen Anne's well-known influence with the king, in order to convey to him, through her, a warning or a remonstrance against proceedings on his part which were calculated to endanger his safety and the peace of the kingdom. I shall quote the poet's words, as without doubt they have a special bearing on the question under discussion. In lines 321-334 Alcestis is made to say :—

> A god ne schulde not thus been a-greuyd
> But of his dede (deite) he schal be stable
> And therto ryghtful and ek mercyable
> He schal nat ryghtfully his yre wreke
> Or he haue herd the tothyr partye speke
> Al ne is nat gospel that is to yow pleynyd
> The god of love hereth manye a tale I-feynyd
> ffor in youre court is manye a losenger
> And manye aqueynte totulour acusour
> That tabourryn in youre eres manye a thyng
> ffor hate or for Ielous ymagynyng
> And for to han with you sum dalyaunce
> Enuye I prere to god yeue hire myschaunce
> Is lauender in the grete court alway :

and again in lines 353-375 :—

> This schulde a ryghtwys lord han in his thought
> And not ben lyk tyrauntis of lumbardye
> That vsyn wilfulhed and tyrannye
> ffor he that king or lord is naturel
> Hym oughte nat be tyraunt and crewel
> As is a fermour to don the harm he can
> He must thynke it is his lige man
> And that hym owith o verry duetee
> Schewyn his peple pleyn benygnete
> And wel to heryn here excusacyouns
> And here compleyntys and petyciouns
> In duewe tyme whan they schal it profre
> This is the sentens of the philysophre
> A kyng to kepe hise lygis in iustise
> * (Withouten) doute that is his offise
> And therto is a kyng ful depe I-sworn
> fful manye an hunderede wyntyr here be-forn
> And for to kepe his lordys hir degre
> As it is ryght and skylful that they be
> Enhaunsede and honoured most dere
> ffor they ben half-goddys in this world here
> This schal he don bothe to pore (and) riche
> Al be that here stat be nat a-lyche.

I submit that, even if it be admitted that the first of these passages is not wanting in appositeness in an argument intended to reason the God of Love out of his wrath, it is impossible to concede appositeness to the second passage. What has the God of Love got to do with the distinctions between rich and poor, or the advancement in rank of his lords ? Why should Love, to whom the gods themselves are sometimes subject, be afraid of any *half-goddys ?* The arguments and appeals in the second passage have been dragged in to the violation of the fitness of things, in respect either to the character of the God of Love or to the circumstances of the fable out of which these arguments and appeals arise. The introduction of a lecture on the duties of a king, expressed in tones at once earnest and solemn, suggests a suspicion that the poet had some special and important end in view. There is nothing unreasonable in such a hypothesis. It would not have been the first, nor would it have been the last, occasion on which the poet took upon himself the *rôle* of political adviser. In the *Parlement of Foules*, as I have shown in my Introduction to that poem,† he seems to have thrown out hints as to what, in his opinion, was the best line of policy to

---

* G.—Which oughtyn *for* withouten.
† See *Chaucer's Minor Poems*, ed. by J. B. Bilderbeck. Bell & Co.

be pursued in relation to the peasants after their great revolt. Moreover, in his *balade* on the *Lack of Stedfastnesse*,* described in Shirley's MS. at Trin. Coll., Camb., as having been " made in hees laste yeeres," and, in Harleian MS. 7333, as having been sent to Richard "in his Castell of Windesore," he again admonishes the king in language that can hardly be misunderstood.

A reference to the events in the reign of Richard II. reveals what obviously were the poet's intentions. In the midst of much general advice to the effect that kings must be just, impartial, and merciful, and that they should be on their guard against flatterers and backbiters, there occur some special warnings, viz., that, instead of headstrong wilfulness, a king should listen to the petitions and attend to the grievances of his people, and that he should respect the rank and rights of the nobility, who should be honoured and promoted according to their due, for, though they may be inferior to him, they, as *half-goddes*, possess a great deal of power.

The sting of the lecture on the duties of a king may be said to lie chiefly in its tail. Under the influence, possibly, of Robert de Vere, Earl of Oxford, for whom he seems to have entertained a great affection, and also of other members of the royal household, the young king had apparently begun to hold exaggerated views of the royal position and power. More particularly, he seems to have resented the influence exercised in the affairs of the State by his uncles and the political party that sustained them, and he conceived it to be his best policy "to raise up a counterpoise to them by promoting and enriching servants of his own " (Stubbs' *Constitutional Hist.*, II., p. 510).

When Richard le Scrope, the Chancellor nominated in Parliament, objected (July, 1382) to Richard's lavish gifts, the king forced him to give up the seals. In 1383 he followed up this assertion of independence by appointing de la Pole, who was the son of a merchant, to the office of Chancellor without any reference to Parliament.† Moreover, he seems to have quarrelled with his uncle, John of Gaunt, who for several years had exercised a most powerful influence in the administration of the State. In 1384, charges of treason were brought against Lancaster,‡ and, though Richard accepted his

---

* See *Chaucer's Minor Poems*, ed. by J. B. Bilderbeck. Bell & Co.
† *Dict. Nat. Biog.*—Richard II.
‡ Walsingham, *Hist. Anglic.* (Riley), II., p. 113.

uncle's explanations, we may infer that he did not do so very willingly, for his youngest uncle, Thomas of Woodstock, Earl of Buckingham, is said to have threatened him with death if he charged his brother with treason.* In the following year (1385), the quarrel appears to have again broken out, and Lancaster, fearing arrest, betook himself to his castle at Pontefract, which he fortified.† A reconciliation was effected between them, and Lancaster accompanied the king in his expedition to Scotland (August, 1385), but Richard was unwilling to take his uncle's advice in respect to the course of military operations, and the unsuccessful character of the expedition was the cause of a *scene* between them.‡

In March, 1385, the king bestowed on his favourite, the Earl of Oxford, the castle and lordship of Queensborough; and on August 6th of the same year he ennobled de la Pole, creating him Earl of Suffolk, though he took care to give on the same day a step in the peerage to his two uncles, Edmund of Langley and Thomas of Woodstock, whom he created Duke of York and Duke of Gloucester respectively. It was not long before the jealousy and anger caused by the policy of the king found strong expression.§ In the Parliament of 1386 (October), the king was confronted with a demand for the dismissal of his Chancellor and Treasurer. His ministers were accused of withdrawing him from the society of the barons, and this accusation formed one of the charges brought against the Chancellor, Suffolk, in the Merciless Parliament of 1388.‖

That the king was disinclined to accept suggestions which had the appearance of being dictated to him, or, in other words, that he was disposed to exhibit that "*wilfulhed*" against which the poet warns him, is clear from what has been said, and is again illustrated by his reply to the Parliament of 1385 (October 20th–December 6th). When requested to sanction an annual examination of the affairs of

---

* Walsingham, *Hist. Anglic.*, II., p. 115.

† Walsingham, *Hist. Anglic.*, II., p. 126: "Juvene rege et juvenibus ejus complicibus in mortem illius (*i.e.*, Lancaster) conspirantibus."

‡ Walsingham, *Hist. Anglic.* II., pp. 131, 132.

§ Richard, in reference to the grant to the Earl of Oxford above referred to, invoked "the curse of God and St. Edward and the King" upon all who should do or attempt anything against his grant. Such a curse would imply that remonstrances against his proceedings had already reached his ears (*Dict. Nat. Biog.*—de Vere).

‖ For the statements in the paragraph see *Dict. Nat. Biog.*—Richard II., Edmund of Langley, Thomas of Woodstock, de la Pole, de Vere.

the royal household, he said he would do so when he pleased; and, to a petition for the declaration of the names of his officers for the year, he replied that he should change them when he pleased.

What has been stated is enough to show that in 1384, 1385, 1386, Richard's proceedings were, in many respects, exactly those against which Alcestis warns the God of Love; and there can hardly be any room for doubt that Chaucer, who was so intimate with the Court, and who was a friend of the Duke of Lancaster, considered it his duty to do what in him lay to check a policy which he must have foreseen would lead to misfortune, or even ruin.

From the beginning of 1387 to the middle of 1389, Richard was practically superseded and was kept in tutelage by the powerful party of Gloucester, who, as the Duke of Lancaster was absent from the country, was the real head of the administration. In May, 1389, Richard, by a *coup d'état*, took the reins of government into his own hands, and, having learnt wisdom by experience, inaugurated a method of administration which was conspicuous for its prudence and moderation. The country enjoyed peace for several years, and, outwardly at least, the king refrained from a policy of revenge. As Stubbs says, "For eight years Richard governed England as, to all appearance, a constitutional and popular king" (*Const. Hist.*, II., p. 526).

As, during the first of the aforesaid periods, that of Gloucester's ascendency, Richard was little more than a king in name, and as, during the second of these periods, he ruled constitutionally, Chaucer's lecture on the duties and responsibilities of a king cannot be held to apply to either of them. It follows that we must place the earlier version of the Prologue of the Legend in one of the three years, 1384 1385, 1386.

It is, I think, possible to get even nearer to the exact date. I am inclined to reject the year 1386, for by that time the king would seem to have committed himself irretrievably to the mistaken policy against which the poet would appear to have warned him.*

---

* He seems to have been unable to free himself from the fascination or influence of Robert de Vere, whom, towards the end of 1385, he created Marquis of Dublin, much to the annoyance of members of the baronage who were thereby superseded in rank. According to Walsingham (*Hist. Anglic.*, II., p. 160), the king countenanced de Vere's efforts to obtain a divorce from his wife Philippa, a granddaughter of Edward III. This scandal was probably in an acute stage in the latter part of 1386.

An earlier date would be more probable. Acquainted as he must have been with the temper of the king, the character of some of his favourites, and the general tendencies of the new policy, Chaucer, it may be presumed, determined to take advantage of what was at once a compliment to and a commission from the queen to convey to the king a strong and *timely* hint of the dangers that might attend a blind and unqualified adhesion to the policy which he seemed disposed to pursue.

On the other hand, in the year 1384 not very much harm appears to have been done by the new policy, and this date is perhaps too early for our purpose, as the poet was probably engaged on the *House of Fame* during that year. The date 1385 seems to be the most likely one of the three mentioned. It was about the middle of that year that the king must have decided on ennobling de la Pole, for he was created Earl of Suffolk on August 6th, 1385. To many of the great nobles the promotion of de la Pole was the elevation of an upstart. It was in the same year that John of Gaunt fortified himself against arrest in his castle in Pontefract. These events perhaps inspired the poet's recommendation that the king should "kepe his lordys hir degre"; that they should be "*enhaunsede* and honoured" as "half-goddys"; and that he should—

>   Nat ryghtfully his yre wreke
>   Or he haue herd the tother party speke* (G. 324, 325).

The identification of 1385 as the date of the composition of the earlier Prologue seems to be confirmed by other considerations. It is surely something more than a mere coincidence that the scene of the dream-fable is laid in the month of May, and that *nineteen* has been selected as the number of the ladies attending on the God of Love or the queen who accompanies him, and as the number of the ladies whose names are commemorated in the *balade*. The introduction of a May scene may be a favourite device with poets, but it is worthy of note that Anne was born in May. As she was born on May 11th, 1366,† she would have been just *nineteen* years of age in May, 1385; and here we have two facts which it is not unlikely that the poet who intended to pay the queen a compliment would have turned to account.

* These lines are omitted in the revised version of the Prologue.
† *Dict. Nat. Biog.*—Anne.

I submit, then, that the Prologue in its earlier form may be referred to May, 1385, and I shall now proceed to discuss the question of the date of the composition of the revised form of the Prologue.

It has been shown that Chaucer's own statements in the earlier form of the Prologue point to the inference that work on the poem was to be co-extensive with his life. Moreover, evidence has been advanced to prove that Chaucer revised not only the Prologue, but most of the legends. That the version of the Prologue and of the legends found in the Cambridge University MS. was not intended for publication or presentation to the Court is improbable, and it is only open to us to hold that the text of the poem in this MS. represents, not a rough draft of the poem, but the draft—perhaps an imperfect one—of the poem as originally written for presentation to the Court. These considerations do not in any way amount to proof that the second form of the Prologue is to be assigned to a date much later than the earlier form, but they at least suggest the view that the dates of the composition of these Prologues were separated by some interval of time, and that circumstances had arisen which led the poet to decide on revision. It seems possible to indicate some of these circumstances.

In the first place, attention will be drawn to the evidence provided by the second form of the Prologue. The revised Prologue is distinguished from the earlier form by presenting several passages which, presumably, are intended as compliments to the queen. See lines 50–53, 56–60, 83–96, 270–275, 296–299. In these passages, the notes of gratitude and devotion are unmistakable, and we may fairly conjecture that they were evoked by some recent and signal proof of her gracious appreciation of the poet. If we remember that the king had not acted on the wise advice suggested by the poet in the earlier form of the Prologue; that his *wilfulhed* brought about a powerful combination of some of the nobles under the leadership of Gloucester, who, during the years 1387, 1388, and a part of 1389, was virtually at the head of the Government, and had reduced the king to a condition of tutelage; that Chaucer himself apparently shared in the disasters consequent on the king's shortsighted obstinacy, for in December, 1386, he was deprived both of the office of Comptroller of the Customs of Wool and of the office of Comptroller of the Petty Customs in the Port of London, which he had held for some years;* that, in 1387, the poet appears to have lost his wife,* and that, in 1388, he seems to have been under the necessity of relinquishing his pensions;* we must come to the conclusion that the period under reference was one in which Fortune was most unkind to Chaucer, and in which the material outlook for him was most gloomy. However, by a *coup d'état* in May, 1389, the young king regained his power, and, on July 12th in the same year, Chaucer received the apparently valuable appointment of Clerk of the King's Works in connection with certain palaces and royal residences.* This sudden accession of prosperity after a period of adversity must have been extremely grateful to the poet, who perhaps was indebted to the queen for this mark of royal favour, and the conviction cannot be resisted that his feelings of gratitude and loyalty found early expression in the revised form of the Prologue of the *Legend of Good Women*.

In the revised form of the Prologue, a long passage (152-174) has been interpolated in which the poet, in symbolical language, appears to refer to the new era of peace and prosperity—so long desired and so necessary in the interests of the country—which seemed to be assured to England by the new policy of the king who, in May, 1389, had taken the administration of affairs into his own hands. Warned by his past experiences, the king determined to rule constitutionally, as we may see from his proclamation issued on the 8th May, 1389.† As examples of the wisdom and moderation of the policy by which he was now guided may be mentioned his abstention from taking revenge in respect to the proceedings of the chief actors in the late Merciless Parliament, his arranging a three years' truce with France, Spain, and Scotland, and his assenting ‡ (March, 1390) to a body of rules for the management of the business coming before the Privy Council, among which we find a rule forbidding all gifts by the king without the assent of the king's uncles and of the Chancellor or of two of them. Further, in the interests of the poor rather than of the rich, an ordinance against *maintenance* was passed early in 1390, and this includes a prohibition of the old custom of giving livery of company.

* See Furnivall, *Trial Forewords*, pp. 25-27.
† See his proclamation, dated 8th May, 1389, in Rymer's *Fœdera*.
‡ See Nicolas, *Proceedings and Ordinances of the Privy Council*, Vol. I., pp. 18a, 18b.

I submit that allusions to these facts are to be found in the following extracts from the passage referred to :—

> (1) And thus thise foweles voide of al malice
> Acordeden to love and laften vice
> Of hate.

Not many years previously (1382), in the *Parlement of Foules*, Chaucer, under the symbolism of birds and their disputes, had indulged in various references to the society and the politics of the day. His readers must have been familiar with the inner meaning of his parable in the aforesaid poem, and there can be little doubt that, in the re-employment of the same symbolism, they would at once have recognised that the poet was referring to the healing of differences among the political parties of the period under reference, and the return to loyalty on the part of those who, with the Duke of Gloucester, had been in opposition to a king who now showed himself energetic enough and wise enough to assume control of the administration.

> (2) Yet pitee thurgh his stronge gentil myght
> For-gaf and mad mercy passen ryght
> Thurgh Innocence and ruled curtesye
> But I ne clepe (F. ins. 'yt') nat Innocence folye
> *Ne fals pitee for vertue is the mene
> As etike saith in swich maner I mene.

The interpretation of these lines in relation to their context is a matter of some difficulty, if we confine our attention merely to the fable pure and simple. On the other hand, in the light of the hypothesis that the poet is lauding the moderation and forgiving spirit which characterised the new policy of the king, the lines acquire the fullest significance. The same theme animates the passage towards the end of Gower's *Confessio Amantis*,† in which he eulogises the king, and also the lines of Richard de Maidstone : ‡

> Adde quod in miseros semper solet hic misereri
> Nec habet ultrices rex pius iste manus
> Quot mala quot mortes tenero sit passus ab ævo
> Quamque sit inultus Anglia tota videt.

---

* In his reference to Aristotle and the golden mean Chaucer perhaps is paying Gower the compliment of reminding the king of his treatment of this matter in *Conf. Amant.*, Bk. VII.

† See Pauli, III., pp. 375-377.

‡ Richard's Reconciliation with the City of London, 1393, in Wright, *Political Poems and Songs*, Vol. I., p. 283.

(3) Welcome somer oure gouernour and lorde
And Zepherus and Flora gentilly
Yaf to the floures softe and tenderly
Hire swoote breth and made hem for to sprede.

Here the poet seems to announce the arrival of a summer-time of peace and prosperity in the land after a period of discontent and misfortune.

Moreover, it is worthy of notice that, in the revised form of the Prologue, several important and significant changes have been made in the passage dealing with the duties of a king. The *wilfulhed* of G. 355 disappears; the lines (360-364) in which the king is informed that it is incumbent on him to listen to the grievances and petitions of his people have been excised; lines 368, 369, which darkly convey some threat of retribution, have also been cancelled; and lines 370-374, which advise the king to give proper consideration to the rights and privileges of "his lordes," have undergone a most significant revision. In brief, a careful comparison of lines 373-390 in the revised Prologue with the corresponding passage (lines 353-376) in the earlier version reveals a striking difference in the author's point of view. The note of admonition in the latter gives place to a note of admiration in the former, which reads like a compliment to a king whose acts and policy are in strict accordance with the ideal of kingship presented by the poet.

Again, it is perhaps not without significance that the poet has modified the description of the head-dress worn by the God of Love (G. 160, 161, F. 228-231). In the earlier version, prominence had been given to the presence of the lilies in the garland on his head, and, in this connection, it is perhaps important that we should remember that a short truce with the French expired on the 1st May, 1385; that, on the expiration of this truce, the French sent troops into Scotland, and that, as an invasion of England was expected from this quarter, a large army was levied which the young king commanded in person,* and with which he entered Scotland on 6th August, 1385. Now, it is remarkable that in the revised form of the Prologue we hear nothing about the lilies, and the explanation of this is probably to be found in the fact already stated, that a three years' truce had been concluded with France in 1389.

In view of the various considerations above stated, the revised

* Walsingham, *Hist. Anglic.*, II., pp. 127, 129, 131.

form of the Prologue may be referred to the month of May, 1390, by which time the king's subjects would have had ample opportunity of judging of the sincerity of his intentions as expressed in the proclamation of the 8th May, 1389.

The hypothesis that the second form of the Prologue is to be referred to the year 1390 finds confirmation in other considerations.

As is well known, Chaucer, in his Prologue to the *Tale of the Man of Law*, refers to the character and contents of his *Legend of Good Women*, which he therein designates the *Seintes Legende of Cupyde*. Inasmuch as he enumerates several good women whose lives do not occur in the Legend, and omits the names of Cleopatra and Philomela, whose legends are included, and in view, moreover, of the fact that the poem terminates abruptly, and seems never to have been completed, we must infer that what he puts into the mouth of the Man of Law refers not to work accomplished and in existence, but to plans that he had in view. It is evident that, while he was engaged on the *Tale of the Man of Law*, the subject of the Legend was also occupying his mind, and it may be reasonably supposed that he was planning the prosecution or the completion of his work. The question consequently arises whether there were any special circumstances which might have evoked from Chaucer a declaration of his intentions in regard to the *Legend of Good Women*. The answer to this question bears on the relations of Chaucer and Gower, which I reserve for fuller treatment in another paper. It is, I believe, a matter of general acceptance that Chaucer refers to Gower's *Confessio Amantis* in the Prologue to the *Tale of the Man of Law*, and I think I am in a position to offer several strong reasons in support of this view.

The recent researches of Mr. G. C. Macaulay [*] have enabled him to fix precisely the year 1390 as the date for the completion of the first version of Gower's great poem. If, then, there is an allusion to this poem in the Prologue to the *Tale of the Man of Law*, it follows that this Prologue could not have taken its present shape before 1390, and it would be fair to assume that it was about the same date that Chaucer was considering the plan of his *Legend of Good Women*, and revising those portions of the poem that he had already written.

There are, moreover, other considerations which tend to confirm

---

[*] Works of John Gower, II., p. xxi.

the hypothesis that the second form of the Prologue of the Legend was written after Gower's *Confessio Amantis*, and after, or at the same time as, the Prologue to the *Tale of the Man of Law*.

If we compare the two forms of the Prologue to the *Legend of Good Women*, we find that Chaucer has omitted in the second cast every reference to his age which is found in the earlier cast (see lines 258-263, 314-315, 400-401). What seems to me to be the true significance of this change, so far as I know, has never before been pointed out.* If we do not look beyond Chaucer's own poem, the reasons for the change are by no means obvious; but they become intelligible when we consider the scheme of the *Confessio Amantis* and Gower's remarks in the 8th book with reference to Chaucer. The plot of the *Confessio Amantis*—if such a word as *plot* can be here used with propriety—turns on the vain efforts of an old man to gain the affections of the lady whom he loves, and Gower, with considerable self-assurance, tells the story in the first person, and thus identifies himself with the antiquated lover. The poet, in his Prologue to the first version, says that he proposes to—

> . . . write in such a maner wise
> Which may be wisdome to the wise
> And play to hem that list to play; (Prol. 82-5.)

and his representation of himself as a lover who is advanced in years may have been intended to provide some of the leaven of enlivening humour for the dough of "wisdome to the wise." If this was his intention, it is hardly possible to admit that the result was a success. I submit that what I cannot but characterise as Gower's eminent misadventure was in itself enough to warn Chaucer against the repetition of a similar error in his own artistic work, and may have suggested to him the wiser course of eliminating such an incongruity as that of making an old man sing of love. But this is not all. Gower, after all his foolery at his own expense, concludes his story with various moral reflections about the folly of dotards, and he makes Venus tell him—

> . . . turne thou in my court no more
> But go there vertue moral dwelleth
> Where ben thy bokes, as men telleth,
> Whiche of long time thou hast write. (Pauli, iii. p. 373.)

---

* B. ten Brink (*Englische Stud.*, xvii., p. 14) argues from the presence of references to Chaucer's age in G., and their absence in the other texts, that the form of Prologue in G. is the later.

He here seems to accept Chaucer's epithet of the "moral Gower" as an appropriate description of his *rôle* in life, and almost immediately proceeds to speak of his great contemporary, to whom, at the bidding of Venus, he is to convey a message:—

>Forthy now *in his daies olde*
>Thou shalt him telle this message
>That he *upon his later age*
>To sette an end of all his werke
>*   *   *   *
>Do make his testament of love. (Pauli, iii. p. 375.)

The passage from which these lines have been extracted has been described as highly complimentary to Chaucer: it might be held that malice lurks in the lines. Whatever may have been Gower's intentions, or his real feelings towards Chaucer, the fact remains that he describes his brother poet as an old man, and advises him to make his testament of love, and this advice is offered just after Gower himself has acknowledged the folly of an old man having any dealings with the Court of Venus. Whether Chaucer took offence is an open question, but there can be little doubt that he recognised the *reductio ad absurdum* of the position in which Gower had placed him, and his recognition of this probably reinforced his determination to eliminate all references to old age which his artistic sense also condemned.

There are two other matters which may be advanced in support of the hypothesis that the revision of the Prologue of the Legend was subsequent to, or contemporary with, the appearance of the Prologue to the *Tale of the Man of Law* and of the Tale itself in its extant form.

In the first place, I have stated in an earlier section that, with one exception, there are in G. no headings to the legends in what appears to be a contemporary hand, but that, in some of the other MSS., the headings of Legends I.—VI. describe the heroines as *martyrs*. Now, in the Prologue to the *Tale of the Man of Law*, Chaucer renames his Legend—perhaps in a spirit of mischief and with a touch of irony—the *Seintes Legende of Cupyde*. His language suggests the impression that he was not disinclined to regard the poem as a burlesque of the *Legenda Aurea*, or other similar collection of the lives of saints and martyrs. Whether the poet was in earnest or in game, it is obvious that the term *martyr* is in keeping with the new title of the poem, and it is impossible to resist the conviction that he was as much the author of the former as he was of the latter, and that he was revising the legends at the same time as he was writing the Prologue to the *Tale of the Man of Law*.

In the second place, in comparing the lists of Chaucer's works given in the earlier and in the revised Prologue (see G. 406-418, F. 417-428), we find that, in the latter, the poet has omitted his reference to his translation of *The Wrechede Engendrynge of Mankynde*. An almost obvious explanation of this omission seems to be found in the hypothesis that the poet had decided to utilise the material of this work by incorporating adapted parts of it with other works. As Professor Lounsbury* has pointed out, several of the stanzas in the *proem* of the *Tale of the Man of Law*, and in the Tale itself, embody translations from Pope Innocent's *De contemptu mundi sive de miseria conditionis humanæ*, which is probably the work to which Chaucer refers, while the *Pardoneres Tale* reveals other obligations to the same work. If Chaucer had decided that his translation should no longer have an existence as a separate work, we cannot fail to connect this decision with his plans for the *Tale of the Man of Law*. In the omission of his reference to this translation, we seem to have another link connecting the *Legend of Good Women* with the *Tale of the Man of Law*, and a consequent confirmation of the view that the second form of the Prologue to the former poem cannot be assigned to an earlier date than 1390.

By various and independent trains of reasoning, we have arrived at practically the same result, that the revision of the Prologue of the Legend was made not earlier than 1390. We should perhaps be justified in assigning the revision to the year 1390 in view of the following reasons :—(1) It seems probable that Chaucer would have taken the first opportunity offered to him of eulogising the king and the queen after he had entered, in July, 1389, on the duties of his new appointment, and, if his legends were of the nature of an annual tribute payable in May, he would have had to revise his earlier Prologue before the month of May, 1390. (2) It also seems probable that Chaucer would have taken notice of Gower's *Confessio Amantis* (a copy of which must have been presented to the Court, and therefore was probably accessible to Chaucer) immediately after its appearance rather than at a later period. (3) It has been shown

* *Studies in Chaucer*, Vol. II., pp. 329-334.

that the earlier Prologue is probably to be referred to the May of 1385, and in view of the lines (G. 542-5)—

> At Cliopatre I wele that thow begynne
> * * * * *
> And with that word of slep I gan a-wake
> And *ryght thus* on myn legende *gan I make,—*

it may be inferred that at least the *Legend of Cleopatra* was presented to the Court on the same occasion as the Prologue. Now, the period from May, 1385, to May, 1390, includes *six* months of May, and, as has been stated in another part of this dissertation, there is no evidence of a revision of any of the legends after the *sixth*—that of Ariadne. In this we have a coincidence in numbers which is consistent at once with the hypothesis that the poet contributed at least one legend a year, and also with the hypothesis that the legends underwent revision at the same time as the Prologue.

Before I conclude this discussion, I would remark that the theory herein advanced offers a point of view which enables us to comprehend Chaucer's reasons for revising the Prologue of the Legend, and also to understand why there is such a striking difference in tone and treatment between the two Prologues. The earlier Prologue embodies a lecture which, breathing a spirit of concern and anxiety, is directed against the follies and miscalculations of the administration. If, then, the Legend was undertaken as a compliment to the queen, and, when completed, was to be presented to her, it would be necessary for the poet, if he did nothing else, to revise the language of a lecture which the new methods of government, initiated in May, 1389, had rendered irrelevant. He would naturally have taken advantage of the opportunity in order to make other changes. As the *rôle* of political adviser assumed by him in 1385 was difficult, and not unattended with danger, he carefully guarded himself against giving offence by a cautious and consistent employment of the device—frequently employed for similar purposes—of translating the solid realities of life into the shadows of dreamland. In 1390, a change had come over the spirit of his dream. In the revised Prologue—in which, as already indicated, the dreamer frequently lapses into the man awake—the poet employs less indirect methods for the expression of his feelings of admiration, loyalty, and gratitude.

The suggestion that the earlier Prologue was written in 1385,

Chaucer's Legend of Good Women

and the later in 1390, provides a working hypothesis which has been shown to offer a reasonable explanation of much that is found in the Prologues, and of many of the difficulties surrounding their existence. I am not aware that there are any serious objections to this hypothesis to which an adequate answer could not be forthcoming.*

To sum up the results of this investigation. Chaucer, having been called upon by his Sovereign to set to work on a *Legend of Good Women*, commenced his poem in 1385, and possibly wrote at least one legend every year. In 1390, in order to pay a high compliment to a king whose administration was winning golden opinions, and to a queen who had shown him signal marks of favour, he revised both the Prologue and the legends that he had already written. At the same time, the plan of the work apparently underwent some modification, for, instead of the number of good women whose legends he should write being unlimited, the number was now limited, and he had instructions to finish a task which under the older conditions was but the labour of Sisyphus.

* Much of the above discussion involves what I submit is a satisfactory reply to the arguments of ten Brink in support of his view that G. presents the later form of the Prologue (*Englische Studien*, xvii., 18, 19). One of these arguments perhaps requires special notice. The statements in lines 554-557, in what this eminent scholar termed the *Vulgata*, appear to be inconsistent with the fact that only eighteen ladies are mentioned in the *balade*, or the fact that the poem includes the legends of ladies not named in the *balade*. The whole passage in which these lines occur is absent in G., which is therefore free from the inconsistency. According to ten Brink, the absence of this inconsistency is more consistent with the theory of revision than the interpolation of the inconsistency. Such an argument, if associated with more direct evidence, might help to strengthen or confirm this evidence: in itself it can carry no weight. An adequate reply is that the adoption of ten Brink's theory involves far more serious inconsistencies than those it removes, for the theory cannot explain how it is that so many of the *Vulgata* readings are superior to the corresponding readings in G.; or how that in G. the name of Alcestis is prematurely introduced in the *balade*; or why Chaucer should be expected to undertake a heavier task in place of a lighter one. If the usual interpretation that is placed on the lines under reference is the right one, it is impossible to deny the inconsistency. Possibly, Chaucer may have been guilty of an oversight, for the whole passage in which the lines occur reads like a hurriedly expressed afterthought.

Possibly, the objection urged by Dr. Köppel (*Englische Studien*, xvii., 199), in respect to a suggestion of ten Brink's, may be held to apply equally to my view that the second form of the Prologue to the L.G.W. was written after, or about the same time as, the Prologue to the *Tale of the Man of Law*. In the eyes of some, it might be fatal to this view that, in spite of what the Man of Law said

Appendix.—Some Doubtful Readings.

483   G. That he schal charge hise seruantys by ony weye.

In 493, F.T.B.Th.A.P. confirm this reading. A good reading, and possibly the correct one, is found in R.a. :—

That he hys seruantes charge by eny way.

560   F. Thanne thow knowest good wommen alle.

T.B.Th.P. agree with F., while R.a. (*that* for *thanne*) insert *and* after *knowest*. The A. reading, *Than thow knowest that ben good wommen all*, is heavy, and places the inflexional part of *knowest* in one of the stress-positions, which, though not without analogy, is unusual in dissyllables. The line apparently commences with a monosyllabic measure, and should read: *Than thow knowest goode wommen alle*, as in γ. with *knowest* for *knewest*.

641   G. Among the ropis rennyth the scherynge hokys.

For *rennyth*, F.B.T. *and* ; Th. *ran* ; A.P. *than*, *thenn* ; R.a. corrupt, but read *raf, rase*. The F.B.T. reading does not appear to make any sense. G. *rennyth* seems sound enough ; the tense is consistent

about the story of Canace, this name should be retained in the *balade*. In this case, *Galfridus aliquando dormitat* is a plea that cannot be urged. There is ample evidence that the *balade* had been carefully revised, for not only has the refrain in each strophe been altered, but the poet has modified the fifth and sixth lines of the third strophe, in which Canace's name occurs. In reply, I might urge what has already been suggested, that Chaucer reserved to himself some liberty of selection, and did not consider himself bound to write legends on all the ladies mentioned in the *balade*. But even if, with Bech (*Anglia*, V., 371 ff.), we take the extreme view that the *balade* contains the names of all the intended subjects of the legends, the difficulty is not insuperable. I suggest that Chaucer may have deliberately placed himself in a dilemma in a spirit of intellectual stubbornness characteristic of a certain order of great minds. His friends and critics may have thought that he was stultifying himself. Either the story of Canace must be told, in spite of what the Man of Law had said about it, or, by withdrawing Canace's name, he must lay himself open to a charge of carelessness or ignorance of his *Ovid* in having introduced her name. Chaucer probably knew his way out of the dilemma. He had said that he would not write

"Of thilke wikke example of Canace ; "

he did not say that he would tell no story of *a* Canace. In the light of the fact that he has glorified this name by selecting it for his heroine in the beautiful "half-told tale" of the Squire, I think it is a fair conjecture that Chaucer was meditating the creation of a Canace of his own.

with the context, and the trisyllabic measure is effective, the cesural pause coming after the third measure.

659 G. Myn worshepe in this day thus have I lorn.

So F.T.B.Th.; but *day* may have been caught from the preceding line. R.a.A. read, *My worshyp in thys world thus haue I lorn,* which seems to be a better reading.

815 G. And ek so glad that þt sche was escapid.
R. And eke so glad of that she was ascaped.

F.T.B.Th.A.a. (*so glad that she*) are metrically defective. R. is unsupported. Possiby 'þt' in the G. reading has been miswriten for *yit* (see 1538 below). *Yet* makes good enough sense: Thisbe was terribly frightened and also rejoiced that yet—in spite of her fright—she had escaped.

837 G. Myn biddyng hath yow slayn as in this cas.

F.T.B.Th.R. *byddyng,* but this form was perhaps influenced by the word *bidde* in the following line, and miswritten for *byding* or *biding,* which is the reading in A.a.Ff., while γ. reads *hyding.* Pyramus is complaining, *not* that he had invited Thisbe to come to a dangerous place, but that he had been so dilatory in his own movements (see 840, 1).

903 R.a. That in oon graue I-fere we moten ly.
A. That in a graue we mote bothe lye.

Ff. (*one* for *a, motton* for *mote*) confirms A. The latter reading is to be preferred, as *I-fere* is usually found at the end of a line, and is trisyllabic (see *L.G.W.* 1828, and *Second Nonnes* T. 380).

1091 *Massynger,* or *messager,* being a trisyllable, with a secondary accent on the third syllable, the plural inflexion probably does not make an additional syllable. For this reason, the reading of T.—confirmed by R.A.—is possibly correct: *And commanded hir messagers to go.*

1099 G. He neuere at ese was betyr in al hese lyve.

This reading is sound enough metrically, if it be remembered that *neuere* is probably a monosyllable when preceding a vowel. The chief objection to the reading lies in the order of its words. Chaucer would appear to have modified this (see p. 38), but it is not easy to decide which of the two following readings in the other MSS. embodies his emendation:

F.B.A. He neuer better at ese was his lyue.
T.R. P.γ.Rl. He neuere bettre at ese was in his lyue.

The latter reading gives the better metrical balance.

1210 G.F.T.A.B., *this lady ride*, which is ungrammatical. The correct reading seems to have been preserved in R.α.—*thus lat I ryde*.

1238 G. And tok hym for husbonde and become his wyf.

This line is hypermetrical in all the MSS. The first *and* may have been caught from 1236, and its omission would improve the line.

1338 G. And seyde o swete cloth whil Iuppiter it leste
1339   Tak now my soule and brynge it of this onreste.

As regards 1338, F.T. (*is* for *it*) B.Th.P.Rl.γ. agree with G., while R.A.α. omit *swete*. As regards 1339, T.Th.γ. read, *Take my soule vnbynde me of this vnreste*; P.Rl. ins. *and* after *soule*; R.α. ins. *now* after *take*. These two lines are a close translation of Virg. *Æn.*, iv., 651, 2.

> Dulces exuviæ, dum fata Deusque sinebant,
> Accipite hanc animam meque his exsolvite curis;

and it is an open question whether Chaucer was not here experimenting on the artistic effects of lines of six measures, for the former line as it stands in most of the MSS. is undoubtedly such, and the latter line, if *soule* (O.E. *sawol*, a strong femin.) is dissyllabic, may also be regarded as hexametric as it stands in G. or R.α., or even in T.Th.P.Rl.γ. If—see ten Brink, *Chaucers Sprache*, 269—the *e* in *me* can be taken as undergoing elision before *of*, the second line must be regarded as normal in the case of the R.α. and of the T.Th.γ. readings.

1375 G. With thyn obeysaunce and humble cheere.

This is the reading of the best MSS., and seems to be sound, *with* being taken as a monosyllabic first measure. A. and P. insert a second "thyn" before *humble*, but this entails a dislocation in the usual accentuation of *obeysaunce*.

1382 The reading of G. *sekte*—confirmed by α.—is probably correct. For this use of *secte*, see *Clerke's Tale* 1115—whos (wyf of Bathe) lyf and al hir *secte* god mayntene. *Sleighte* in F.B., *seite* in T., *set* in R.A., are obvious misreadings.

Chaucer's Legend of Good Women

1538 G. As wolde god that þt I hadde geue.
       F. As wolde god that I hadde I-yive (T.B.Th.).

A. reads *As wold almychti god that I had geue*, but *had geue* is not confirmed by the *hadde yeve* or *hadde I-yive* of the older MSS. Perhaps we may find the true reading in G., if we substitute *yet* for 'þt,' the latter word being obviously a copyist's error. The emendation suits the context, and involves little more than the change of a single letter, *y* for þ. The letters *y* and þ seem to have been frequently confounded by the scribes—see 436 (G. *the* for *ye*), 517 (R. *thys* for *yis*), 1767 (G. *yit* for *that*), 1883 (R. *look ye* for *loke*þ), 2088 (G. *the* for *ye*).

1659 G. As euere in loue a thef and traytour he was.

This reading is nearly the same as in R.*a*. (*a thyef traytour*), γ. (*a theeff a traytour*), β. (*traytour and theffe*). In G. and γ. we have a trisyllabic fourth measure, which is not without analogy, but the reading in β. gets rid of this, and merits consideration. F.T.B.Th.A. read *a cheve* (*chief*) *traytour*, which is evidently most unsatisfactory editing, weak in expression and poor in rhythm.

1721 F. And softe wolle sayeth our boke that she wroght.

That (found in G.T.B.) is obviously a copyist's error, and is omitted in R.*a*.β.γ., which, however, read *oure boke seyth*. *Wolle* is dissyllabic (see *Cant. T.*: *Pard T.* Prol. 120 and line 582), and its final *e* may, in the R.*a*.β.γ. reading, perhaps be preserved from elision before *oure* by the pause. I would suggest the following slight emendation, which brings rhetorical stress and metrical stress into line: *And softe wolle seith our bok she wroghte.*

1803 G. That hast hire by the throte with a swerd at herte.

For *hast*, F.T.B.Th. read *hath*; R. *holdeth*; A.*a*.β. *hold, holde*. Obviously the G. reading involves a slight error of *s* for *l* in *hast*, which should be *halt*, third person singular of *holden*.

1837 Read *Tarquyn*, a dissyllable, as in 1863 (T.R.A.β.γ.).

1839 F.B. The woo to telle hyt were impossible.
       A. The wo to tellen were an inpossible.

R.*a*.β. confirm A. The reading of F.B. is possibly a bit of editing, as the line in T. is defective—*The wo to tell were impossible*. The reading in A. is similar in expression to other passages in Chaucer,

8

e.g. Cant. T.: *Wif. B.* Prol. 688—*For trusteth wel it is an impossible*; also *Troil. Cres.*, III., 524, 5.

>And for to ben in ought espyed there
>That wiste he wel an impossible were.

1881 F. That so grete feythe in al the londe he ne fonde.
   R.*a*. Nat so gret feyth in all that he ne (*a*. om. *ne*) fonde.

T.Th.B. resemble F., while A.β.γ. resemble R. with *that* for *nat*, an obvious error. *The londe* in F. is hypermetrical, and has probably been caught from the preceding line. R. seems to offer the only sound reading. In G. the line is wanting.

2092 G. Than that I suffered gilt(e)les yow sterve.
   F. Then that I suffred your gentilesse to sterue.

β. confirms G., while A.γ. read *yow giltles to sterue*. T.B.Th. agree with F., whose reading, possibly, is an instance of editing. It is not only the rank of Theseus that appeals to Ariadne, but also the fact that he is to lose his life through no fault of his own (see lines 1979-1982). The reading of G.β. requires only a modification of the spelling of *giltles*, which is trisyllabic (see line 1982, etc.).

2215 The readings in G.F.T.B.Th. make no sense. The best supported reading, that of A.β., and practically γ. (om. *any*), is—

>For though so be that any bote her come.

2294 For the reading here see p. 43.

2396 R. That may ye fynde yef that hyt lyke yow.

The subjunctive—*lyke*—is confirmed by G.γ., and even B., which in this case is unlike its congeners.

2480 G. Wel and homly and let his shepis dighte.

All the authorities but T.Th. read *homly* (var. sp.), but this hardly makes sense, and has perhaps been influenced in its form by the word *home* in the following line. T. reads *humble*, Th. *hombly*, and *humbly* was probably Chaucer's word.

2487 G. But to hym ferst she wrot and faste she prayede.
   F. But firste wrote she to hym and faste hym prayed.

R. (*unto* for *but to*) β. confirm G., except that they omit the second *she*. T.B.Th. agree with F. The correct reading appears to be—

>But to him first she wrot and fastë preyede.

2583 The reading here should be as in G., *these wemen*, referring apparently to the *Werdys* in 2580.

CENTRAL COLLEGE LIBRARIES
821.17 z-biL
Bilderbeck, James Bourdillon.
Chaucer's legend of good women

3 5075 00099 7628

WITHDRAWN